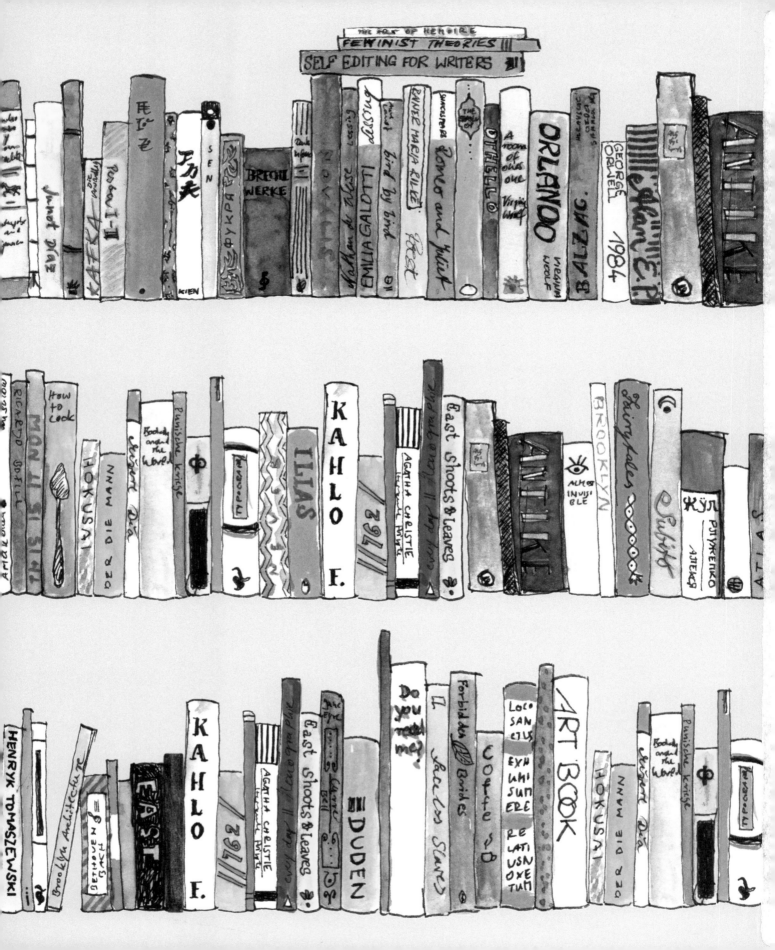

Do You Read Me?

Bookstores Around The World

gestalten

CONTENTS

SURROUNDED BY BOOKS

Bookstores provide us with spaces for reflection and new encounters while making a real contribution towards preserving cultural diversity

Do you read me?" I've come across this question umpteen times. No doubt you have, too. There's something so casual about it that it's easy to ignore altogether. At the same time, its sense of urgency is such that I cannot simply dismiss it. Rather, I see it as a prompt to take a position instead of simply falling back upon the views of others, and to not duck away from other's opinions. As far as I'm concerned, this is all one of the most pressing missions of our time. The Berlin-based book and magazine store do you read me?!, from which this book takes its title, has certainly adopted this mindset.

This photo book draws you into a world that can provide an antidote to pat answers and prevent us from losing sight of the big picture. This requires space for reflection and an opportunity to encounter different realities. Always and everywhere, such spaces are provided for us by bookstores. Indeed, this book could well have been much thicker: there are so many more fantastic bookstores than can be contained in one volume.

The wonderful thing about bookstores is that there's not a single country in the world in which they're simply there to sell books. Their function is not restricted to merely serving the market—you won't find any booksellers who have

geared their business solely towards economic success. They're not driven by money, but by their own attitude. In the process, they make a real contribution towards preserving cultural diversity, actively committed as they are to freedom of expression, which comes coupled with a concern for equal opportunities and tolerance, rather than catering to elitist circles. There are few other places that offer visitors a similar atmosphere in such abundance.

I am fairly familiar with some of the more than 60 bookstores featured in this book. Visiting them is an unforgettable experience. I was particularly taken with the temples to books that you find in Buenos Aires. If I'm ever there, I try to plan enough time for a trip to El Ateneo Grand Splendid on the Avenida Santa Fe, in the Recoleta neighborhood (page 224), which *National Geographic* has just named the most beautiful bookstore in the world. The people of Buenos Aires itself venerate it as a cultural monument—it's simply a must-see, and not just because of its sheer size. It is an emblem of the vibrant culture in the Argentinian capital, which is centered on books and reading, as an unparalleled bookstore with incredibly committed staff, all housed in a building of compelling beauty. It opened as a theater in 1919, with a cinema taking its place a short time later, followed by the

books almost 20 years ago. Despite all of the structural alterations that it has undergone, the building has largely retained its original character and historic charm. I'm not at all surprised that the customers love this place.

The Strand Bookstore on Broadway in New York (page 84) is similarly impressive. This bookstore has been an institution for generations. Founded in 1927 by Benjamin Bass, it remains in the possession of the founding family, who continue to run it with great dedication, aplomb, and success. Sweeping, bright red awnings run around the building, and the famous slogan "18 Miles of Books" is clear to see alongside the name of the store. Checking its veracity would prove difficult, but whatever the case, the sheer abundance of books that you encounter here, away from the hustle and bustle of the city, is enough to take your breath away. More than 2.5 million new and secondhand titles are displayed on the 50,000-square-foot (5,000-square-meter) shop floor, where customers can read, chat, have a laugh, and attend a plethora of events.

Bookstores are places of communication, curiosity, and the new, but they never lose sight of the past. What they do for us, and indeed the whole of society, is easy to take for granted. Some people even contend that bookstores have lost their raison d'être due to the advance of digital technology. Yet booksellers, especially the independent ones, have only grown in creativity and confidence. Their concepts are coming under pressure because reading is in decline in industrial nations, but they are resisting that pressure with great resourcefulness.

I come from a family of booksellers myself: my forebears founded the Poltier-Weeber bookstore in the border town of Lörrach. I also worked for several months as a bookseller during my training at the publishing house Herder Verlag, and, later, towards the end of my university studies, ran the Wagnersche Universitätsbuchhandlung Karl Zimmer in Freiburg. I have always associated bookselling with hard work, but it is also bound up with many wonderful memories: chatting to customers, holding readings, and hosting evening events at which we presented our favorite books. Afterwards, the books often bore red-wine stains where the audience had absentmindedly set their glasses down.

The literary landscape would look very different today were it not for bookstores. This book is intended to celebrate the people who sell books with passion, discover new voices, and uncover old treasures and make them available to the public. In other words, those who welcome the world into their stores. Come along— you'll be glad you did!

Juergen Boos
Director of the Frankfurt Book Fair

BOOKSTORES ARE PLACES OF COMMUNICATION, CURIOSITY, AND THE NEW, BUT THEY NEVER LOSE SIGHT OF THE PAST.

THE DESIRE FOR DISCOVERY

If every bookstore is a fantastical cosmos, then the books are its stars

Anyone who has ever ventured into the boundless expanses of an independent bookstore will be familiar with the feeling that has sparked so many of these stories: the desire for discovery. A new world awaits behind every cover—an undiscovered galaxy upon every shelf.

Do You Read Me? is a literary journey that takes in the most inspiring, remarkable, and successful bookstores that our world has to offer. An incredibly diverse array of ideas, creativity, and commitment thrives here. Whether in a futuristic temple to design in Shanghai, in an antiquarian treasure trove in Tel Aviv, or on a book boat in Burgundy, owners and visitors are united by their deep love for the written word.

Every good book deserves a passionate bookseller: someone who simply lives for the countless stories that, over the pages, enchant, intrigue, challenge, buoy up, inspire, teach, question, and entertain their readers—just like good friends do. The best booksellers know how to recommend the right book for the right situation and to expand the horizons of their customers by directing them towards the next big unknown. As the Kyrgyz author Chinghiz Aitmatov wrote: "Open up books, and you open up yourself."

Do You Read Me? presents bookstores located in private apartments, old factories, and even a boat; stores focused on books for children or dedicated to film or art; and stores devoted entirely to the sea, architecture, or magic. Bestselling author Jen Campbell has some wonderful anecdotes from her time as a young bookseller. In extra guest contributions, business coach Fiona Killackey and *Guardian* books reporter Alison Flood write about the everyday challenges and key success factors for independent bookstores. Juergen Boos, the director of the legendary Frankfurt Book Fair, has provided a lovely foreword. The book also explores the opportunities afforded by the internet and social media, as well as the irreplaceable role that local bookstores can play in ensuring cohesion and the ongoing survival of culture within our cities.

Like any good story, the history of bookstores is taking an unexpected turn.

The number of independent bookstores in the United States is now starting to rise for the first time in 20 years. Small bookstores are holding their own against major chains in Australia, a trend that is also evident among little specialist bookstores in big cities in Germany and the United Kingdom. Booksellers are turning their stores into places for community life and inspiration. They are enriching their neighborhoods with readings, writing workshops, and book signings while providing authors and independent publishers with a platform. At the same time, they are making forays into new realms through spin-off events like small festivals, wine tastings, and craft days for children.

They support schools and universities, run cafés and galleries, and host concerts and launch parties. They are politically active, aesthetically minded, and hugely inspiring, fostering connections within communities, which serve both as their lifeblood and as their vocation. Their comrades-in-arms are every single one of their customers, world-changing books and their authors, visionary publishing houses, graphic artists, typesetters and editors, architects and shop designers, landlords and politicians. Moreover, every visit to an independent bookstore is a manifestation of diversity, character, an authentic sense of community, and hands-on common humanity.

The stores featured in *Do You Read Me?* are just a few examples of the many amazing, creative, and bold bookstores whose very existence enriches our communities, towns, and cities, and the world at large. Their stories continue to be written every day by visionary booksellers. With their lovingly and intelligently curated ranges and events, their commitment, and their unique vision, they form the heart of our invaluable cultural landscapes. This book is for you and all of the other explorers who are making sure that this heart goes on beating.

Marianne Julia Strauss
Co-editor

EVERY VISIT TO AN INDEPENDENT BOOKSTORE IS A MANIFESTATION OF DIVERSITY, CHARACTER, AN AUTHENTIC SENSE OF COMMUNITY, AND HANDS-ON COMMON HUMANITY.

7

GLORIOUS TIMES & DAZZLING WRITING

DO YOU READ ME?! · BERLIN · GERMANY

Challenging the status quo: this bookstore puts the focus on international magazines and independent publishers

RIGHT Magazines of all kinds and formats form the focus of this popular Berlin bookstore.

OPPOSITE Mark Kiessling (pictured) and Jessica Reitz founded do you read me?! amid the print media crisis, yet it remains a success to this day.

We don't really differentiate between books, magazines, glossies, or zines—we only care about whether it works for do you read me?!" says Mark Kiessling, who runs the popular store selling magazines and books in Berlin's Auguststraße, together with Jessica Reitz. Amid galleries, bars, and stylish cafés, the store, which shares its striking name with this book, has gained renown well beyond the German capital as a treasure trove of outstanding contemporary printed products. Its self-appointed mission is to generate publicity for small, independent publishing houses and magazines from all over the world.

The anthracite-colored shelves display the latest issue of *032c* alongside the African collaborative magazine *NICE* and environmental magazine *Atmos*. The selection of books ranges from *We Are the Weather* by Jonathan Safran Foer to *Architektur für die Katz—Schweizer Katzenleitern* from publisher Christoph Merian Verlag. "They're all firm favorites," says Kiessling.

When the visionary book dealer founded his first graphic design studio, Greige, in Berlin in 2001, he was enraptured by the city and its cultural scene. Nonetheless, he felt that something was missing from Berlin, and indeed the rest of Germany. "Of course, there were some great bookstores for designers, architects, and artists, like Pro qm in Berlin, Walther König in Cologne, and Werner in Munich, but interesting magazines, which I often bought abroad, were difficult to →

9

PEOPLE THOUGHT THAT WE WERE CRAZY TO START SPECIALIZING IN THIS FIELD RIGHT IN THE MIDDLE OF A CRISIS FOR PRINTED MEDIA.

TOP The impressive range of magazines is complemented by a smaller selection of books.

LEFT The idea for do you read me?! arose from the owners' own requirements for specialist international magazines.

OPPOSITE do you read me?! seeks to generate publicity for small independent publishing houses and magazines from all over the world.

→ track down," he explains. "My friends and fellow creatives in Berlin and elsewhere across Germany were finding the same thing. At some point, I had the idea of setting up my own store specializing in international magazines." The opportunity arose in 2008. Kiessling had just developed a concept store for a client, and the project involved conducting lots of research in the Berlin-Mitte area. "I had so many ideas and impressions floating around that I thought, 'right, it's now or never.' So I asked Jessica Reitz whether she fancied setting up a 'back to front' bookstore with me, which would focus on magazines and have a smaller selection of books on corresponding themes."

Reitz loved the idea. A bookseller herself, she had already acquired plenty of experience in running a store at the Kulturkaufhaus Dussmann in Berlin, and she shared Kiessling's deep love of print. "Even though some people thought that we were crazy to start specializing in this field right in the middle of a new crisis for printed media, perhaps it was precisely those conditions that helped us to become a Mecca for international magazines so quickly," muses Kiessling. "Digitization and globalization won't stop at bookstores. There's a lot of inevitable change on the horizon, but the great thing is that an analog medium like books or magazines helps us to see the world through different eyes. And each of us can do so at our own, human pace. In that light, bookstores and libraries, like museums, are places that allow you to simply lose yourself. I think that's something very valuable, especially in our increasingly fast-moving times." 📖

FILBOOKS

ISTANBUL · TURKEY

"I love big photobooks and I cannot lie":
an elephant offering culture and coffee
in Istanbul

The aroma of coffee mingles with the smell of freshly printed book pages. Milk and sugar stand alongside the owner's own photography book, *For Birds' Sake*, at Cemre Yeşil Gönenli's bookstore-café. "My bookshop is an elephant," says the photographer, publisher, and owner of FiLBooks. "Fil" literally translates as "elephant" in Turkish. Its name "had to do with our intention of creating a space that is living," he says. "This is how we tried to give a strong soul to our space." Yeşil opened FiLBooks four years ago in Istanbul's trendy Karaköy neighborhood.

Today, his bookstore-café is a popular gathering place for artists, photographers, coffee lovers, and bookworms. Locals and tourists alike flock here to read, have breakfast, and attend author talks, pop-up events, and printing workshops. The café's red velvet cake enjoys cult status, as does its superb selection of art and photography books, which Yeşil is constantly adding to. "Fil is my temporary dream library," he says. "I select the books I want to own, and before someone buys [them], I feel like I am owning them for a while." 📖

LEFT It's no secret that books and coffee are a match made in heaven; FiLBooks serves up both with the most delicious cakes and baked treats.

BOTTOM The turquoise-colored pipes run the length of the entire bookstore, symbolizing the trunk of the eponymous elephant.

OPPOSITE For a number of years, owner Cemre Yeşil Gönenli has run FiLBooks, in the popular Karaköy neighborhood of Istanbul.

13

TOP The two swinging chairs are coveted spots for many customers, who can also snuggle into the couch on the right to read.

LEFT Together with large-format art and photo publications, FiLBooks also sells pretty accessories and stationery.

OPPOSITE If you're having trouble choosing from the selection of cakes, we recommend the glorious red velvet cake.

LIBRAIRIE IMBERNON

MARSEILLE · FRANCE

It would be hard to imagine a more suitable location for this charismatic store, which specializes in books about architecture

TOP Katia Imbernon runs an independent publishing house alongside her architecture-themed bookstore.

OPPOSITE Architect Le Corbusier realized his vision of a vertical city in the form of the Cité Radieuse.

The saying "Show me where you live, and I'll tell you who you are" could almost have been coined for Edition Imbernon, a bookstore located in the UNESCO-protected Cité Radieuse, the striking complex originally designed by Swiss-French architect Le Corbusier in 1952 as social housing. "Our independent, international bookstore carries the best works on 20th-century architecture, design, and art," says Katia Imbernon. She and her husband Jean-Lucien Bonillo, a lecturing professor at the École Nationale Supérieure d'Architecture de Marseille, started out by setting up their own publishing house in 2001. The bookstore followed a year later.

"Our aim was always to create something of quality. In this spot, which is regularly visited by experts and lovers of architecture from every continent and country, we just had to give them the opportunity to acquire beautiful and rare publications, classics and new releases, as well as books with wider distribution." Naturally, Le Corbusier and the →

17

LIBRAIRIE IMBERNON

TOP The UNESCO-protected architectural landmark still draws design aficionados from all over the world.

BOTTOM Katia Imbernon and Jean-Lucien Bonillo publish books on modern architecture under their own imprint, Editions Imbernon.

OPPOSITE Edition Imbernon mainly issues publications on 20th-century architecture, design, and art.

→ avant-garde have their place on the shelves. Imbernon also stocks relevant essays, monographs, and publications about alternative urban development and the humanities. Katia's favorite book—*Fernand Pouillon—Architecte Méditerranéen*, by none other than her husband, Jean-Lucien—has long been out of print. It was the first book the company published, she recalls. Le Corbusier would certainly have been a keen customer. 📖

AS INVITING AS AN OPEN BOOK

LIVRARIA DA VILA · SÃO PAULO · BRAZIL

The internationally celebrated design of this bookstore conceals an incredible educational mission

The shelves of the Livraria da Vila open onto the Alameda Lorena like a gateway to another world. Star architect Isay Weinfeld designed the captivating bookstore, which is one of a whole series of stores of the same name in and around São Paulo. The rotating glass shelves that form the entrance have won accolades from all around the world. Behind them, you'll find yourself surrounded by black bookshelves lining the soft white walls and the stairways, according to the architect's description of the bookstore design. Inside, narrow open spaces connect the different floors and reflect the geometrical dimensions of the building. Low ceilings give the sense of being in an intimate space, while roomy couches offer an inviting place to read.

Yet it's not just the outer packaging that is worthy of a prize; the contents are similarly high-powered. The current owner, Samuel Seibel, has a self-imposed educational mission: "I share this with the Brazilian writer and cartoonist Ziraldo, who is a big hit with kids," says the bookseller. "He once said that 'reading is more important than going to school.' Of course, what he meant by this was that →

21

LEFT The interior of the cubic bookstore was designed by star architect Isay Weinfeld.

OPPOSITE Owner Samuel Seibel (seen on page 21) has the heartfelt desire to make the incredible array of literature accessible to children.

AS FAR AS I'M CONCERNED, BOOKS AND EDUCATION GO HAND IN HAND.

→ a child can't become a good student if he or she doesn't read or has poor comprehension of basic texts. As far as I'm concerned, books and education go hand in hand. In a country like Brazil, my motivation for running a bookshop is to contribute towards the development of education in my country."

The Livraria da Vila stocks over 200,000 titles. The events, most of which are free, include talks, a reading club, and a diverse children's program. Seibel now runs eight bookstores under the Livraria da Vila name in greater São Paulo, plus two more in Paraná. Back in 1985, the first Livraria da Vila, founded by Aldo Bocchini and Miriam Gouvea, embodied an accomplished blend of culture, education, and design. Besides Isay Weinfeld, architects including Dante Della Manna and Grégory Bousquet have designed bookstores for the independent chain. Every

Livraria serves as a gathering place and venue for events, while also acting as a clarion call for a more humane vision. "This technological new world is producing more and more people who lack a connection with the simple life," says Seibel. "Going for a walk in the park, watching a good film, or spending some time at a bookshop is a kind of antidote to the highly questionable quality of life that we have today." And independent bookstores provide the peace, tranquility, and content that can only be found in books. "They are islands of democracy and spaces of tolerance." 📖

CAFEBRERÍA EL PÉNDULO

MEXICO CITY · MEXICO

A dedicated concept promoting cultural cohesion within different neighborhoods of Mexico City now extends to seven bookstores

TOP Out of the box: an enormous palm tree grows majestically up through the roof of the Cafebrería El Péndulo.

OPPOSITE The interior of the store draws the eye upwards, too, with books rising practically to the ceiling.

The palm rises symbolically above the roof of the seventh and youngest Cafebrería El Péndulo in Mexico City. In the same fashion, the brainchild of Eduardo Aizenman and his partners has been flourishing, evolving since the 1990s from a private obsession into a cultural institution. From the very outset, Aizenman says, the aim was to create places where stories write themselves. "When things seem uncertain, either politically or economically, our stores bloom. People seem to find comfort in our place, a sense of home."

Open spaces and free events promote a sense of cohesiveness within the neighborhood. Customers come to browse, read, work, and discuss. Besides classic works of literature, poetry, philosophy, history, and art, the selection concentrates primarily on Spanish-language books. The balance between books and events in each Cafebrería is individually tailored to the local neighborhood. "Books are very compact traveling apparatus," says Aizenman. "They offer a very intimate way to grow infinitely." 📖

TOP Framed by floor-to-ceiling bookshelves, the Cafebrería El Péndulo is a prime spot for reading and working.

LEFT The palm tree towers straight up through the bookstore and into the sunny skies above Mexico City.

OPPOSITE The name Cafebrería is no mere coincidence: the in-house café is a popular gathering place.

27

KOSMOS BUCHSALON

ZURICH · SWITZERLAND

At the heart of a cultural center in Zurich lies a bookstore where customers come to drink in their books as they browse the coffee and savor the wine

The Kosmos cultural center is a somewhat singular little pocket of Zurich that has emerged in recent years between the rather sterile Europaallee and the city's former red-light district along Langstrasse. Its star attractions include an art-house cinema, a French bistro, and the popular Buchsalon. "We're at the heart of the Kosmos cultural center, where various different spaces and programs seep into and enhance one another," explains the all-women team behind the Kosmos Buchsalon. "Our bookstore is all about gauging the zeitgeist. It sells books that have something substantial, unprecedented, or amusing to say or reveal about our times." Offering a literary break from the day-to-day grind, the Buchsalon hosts art evenings, book launches, and workshops that take an in-depth look at the titles in question. Keen readers enjoy leafing through books over coffee or wine in one of the inviting corners of the salon. And every three months, a new literary puzzle is displayed in the store window. This bookstore is both cosmopolitan and out of this world, or, as the singer Jamiroquai would put it, "She's cosmic!" 📖

TOP The Kosmos culture hub houses an art-house cinema, a French bistro, and a much-loved book salon.

OPPOSITE The range focuses on contemporary literature and the latest publications on sometimes-uncomfortable topics.

KOSMOS BUCHSALON

TOP Depending on the time of day, visitors might enjoy a cup of coffee or a glass of good wine as they browse the shelves of the book salon.

LEFT The books and their overarching themes feed the mind, while the in-house bar caters to readers' creature comforts.

OPPOSITE The wide stairs in the entrance area reflect the broad spectrum of offerings within this venue.

31

THE WRITER'S BLOCK

LAS VEGAS · NEVADA · USA

In the world's biggest gambling paradise, this bookstore is committed to education, strange birds, and a hint of glamor

W ho described this as a cultural desert? They can't have known about The Writer's Block, in the heart of Las Vegas. Scott Seeley and Drew Cohen founded the ambitious bookstore in 2014. "Almost five years later, with support from local philanthropist and literary arts patron Beverly Rogers, we expanded into a 3,000-plus-square-foot location featuring over 18,000 unique book titles," say the booksellers. The foyer of the shop on 6th Street now has an espresso bar ideal for sitting and reading. The Writer's Block fulfills its self-imposed educational mandate by offering free creative writing workshops, field trips, and courses in schools. Here, Seeley is also performing his own labor of love: he was one of the co-founders of the New York chapter of the charitable organization 826 National, established by bestselling author Dave Eggers and educator Nínive Calegari to offer free coaching and writing courses. The interior of The Writer's Block has been meticulously designed, down to the finest detail—vital for the survival of an independent bookstore in a city this glamorous. One element is the incredible collection of brightly colored artificial birds that watch over the shop. You can adopt one of them and its story for a couple of dollars. Seeley and Cohen know that if you really commit to literature, you just can't lose. 📖

LEFT AND TOP Spot the bird: brightly colored feathers appear in the unlikeliest of places all over the bookstore.

OPPOSITE Drew Cohen (left) and Scott Seeley (right) now successfully run The Writer's Block at a second site.

THE WRITER'S BLOCK

TOP Restraint has no place in Las Vegas. In this city of glamor, interiors are meticulously styled, down to the very last detail.

LEFT The bird theme pops up everywhere: the shape of the café counter is reminiscent of an oversized birdcage.

OPPOSITE The Writer's Block stocks around 18,000 titles over its 3,200 square feet. It also hosts a range of workshops.

35

BOOKOFF
WARSAW · POLAND

This museum bookstore is a real asset to the Polish capital, with its rare art books and active cultural program

LEFT If you're in the market for rare illustrated art books, you're bound to strike gold among the shelves at Bookoff.

BOTTOM Both Bookoff stores are located in the two-part Warsaw Museum of Modern Art.

OPPOSITE The bookstore is actively involved in various literary festivals and promotes initiatives for the younger generation.

Since 2008, Bookoff has been making a name for itself with its art bookstores at both locations of the Warsaw Museum of Modern Art. Classic and current titles on art, photography, design, and architecture fill the shelves in the main museum building, on the Ulica Pańska, and now the new Museum on the Vistula. "We sell rare art books, which are frequently unavailable elsewhere on the Polish market," explains the Bookoff team. The brains behind the store have also been helping to organize the Warsaw Art Book Fair, the country's biggest art book fair, since 2015. Some 68 local and international publishing houses and artists exhibited here in the first year alone, and their numbers are growing. "The bookstore takes an active part in cultural initiatives by participating in projects organized by the Museum of Modern Art in Warsaw," staffers say. "Since 2009, Bookoff has been cooperating and exhibiting at events such as the Łódź Design Festival, the Photofestival, Fashion Week Poland, The Warsaw Book Fair, and the Culinary Book Fair." Bookoff is also involved in the popular "Fotograficzna Publikacja Roku" competition to find the best photography book of the year, and thus plays its own part in replenishing the art book market.

COOK & BOOK

BRUSSELS · BELGIUM

This bookstore seasons its nine
themed sections with unusual décor
and matching culinary areas

The journey through the nine sections of Cook & Book begins with Batman and Obelix, whose life-size figures flank the entrance to the comics department of this one-of-a-kind Brussels bookstore. Visitors of all ages sit at the communal table in the center, flipping through the huge selection of comics from Belgium and all over the world, covering everything from niche titles to manga. Readers can adjust the lamps themselves, while action figures of all stripes watch the colorful pages from above. The bookstore/restaurant concept extends to eight bookstores and a music department. Each of the nine spaces has an eatery offering lunch and dinner in a striking setting. The building is also home to a publishing house and the biggest outdoor terrace in Brussels, add Déborah Drion and Cédric Legein, who have run Cook & Book since 2006.

A real Airstream caravan shimmers in the travel section and can be rented out for events, be it a meeting, romantic dinner, or children's birthday party. Travel guides and adventure →

TOP Floating books make dinner at this remarkable bookstore a literary event.

LEFT The original Airstream caravan is located in none other than the travel section.

OPPOSITE The ecru-colored Fiat 500 and a superb wine selection are the icing on the cake in the La Cucina gastronomy section.

TOP The visual design of the nine themed areas at Cook & Book has been planned down to the very finest detail.

OPPOSITE Amid the fantastical realms of books, the armchair reminds us that we are still physically in Belgium.

→ stories provide inspiration for your next big trip. Meanwhile, a giant model train set and cute cat chairs transform the children's section into a miniature amusement park. The English literature, nature, and art sections also boast creative interior design. And it goes without saying that the bookstore wouldn't be called Cook & Book without a very special section dedicated to gastronomy, cooking, and eating. "La Cucina" is fitted up like a classic trattoria and whisks visitors away on a dream trip to Italy.

An old Fiat 500 invites young guests to play, while tiles adorn the floors and walls, and the black shelving features marble accents and Latin inscriptions. The big glass wall allows diners to see into the busy kitchen. All around are cookbooks to suit every taste, from classic recipe collections and veggie cookbooks to tomes on wine and beer. There are also accessories, stylish kitchen utensils, and bottles of champagne, which can be quaffed as you leaf through a brand-new illustrated book. 📖

41

COOK & BOOK

TOP A Union Jack, a salon-like atmosphere, and a sudden inexplicable hankering for tea: this is unmistakably the English literature section.

LEFT The English section primarily caters to the non-French-speaking customers of Cook & Book.

OPPOSITE Brightly colored seats, teddy bears, and comic-book lamps transform the children's book section into a miniature playground.

MY TIME AS A BOOKSELLER

They say *once a bookseller, always a bookseller,* and that certainly holds true for me.

Running a bookshop is a curious profession. All at once, you're a business manager, a magician, a therapist, a fortune teller, a children's entertainer, an interior designer, and even, on occasion, a zookeeper. You may think that last one is a stretch, but in Minneapolis there's a bookshop called Wild Rumpus where, as well as books, you'll find their many bookshop pets: a kitten called Eartha, two cockatiels, two chinchillas, several ferrets, three rats (Mrs. Who, Mrs. Which, and Mrs. Whatsit), a chicken called Neil, and a Mexican fireleg tarantula, possibly distantly related to Aragog, who apparently likes puppets and science fiction novels and who goes by the name of Rubeus Hagrid.

I may not have had a bookshop tarantula, but across ten years of bookselling, I became acquainted with many bookshop pets. The first bookshop I worked at was called The Edinburgh Bookshop. As you may have guessed, it's in Edinburgh, Scotland, and when I worked there, we only stocked children's books. This meant parents would frequently leave their offspring while they nipped to the supermarket next door (even though we begged them not to do this), and toddlers would attempt to climb the bookshelves before we coaxed them onto the storytelling mat and read them

perilous rhyming adventures with the help of Teaga, the bookshop owner's Leonberger: a dog so large she resembled a bear. We'd tell the children she was Nana from *Peter Pan*—that she'd jumped straight out of JM Barrie's book one night when no one was watching—and they'd often believe us, asking if they could ride her like a pony, to which we hastily replied: no, please and thank you.

Children were, by far, my favorite part of being a bookseller. Once I left the Edinburgh Bookshop and moved down to London, I worked at Ripping Yarns, an antiquarian bookshop in Highgate, which was owned by Celia Mitchell and opened with the help of Monty Python's Michael Palin and Terry Jones. It has since moved, but at the time, it was the kind of shop you'd expect to find on Diagon Alley, which is to say it looked as though it was held up by magic, and once inside it, you could hardly move. We specialized in 1930s children's books, though we stocked everything from archaeology to zymology, and I remember having a conversation with one of our youngest customers who wanted to know if she could get to Narnia through one of the bookcases. I apologized profusely and said that our bookshelves didn't work for getting to faraway places (before adding that the books themselves could help transport her), and she sighed, looking

wise beyond her years, and said: "That's OK, our wardrobe at home doesn't work for getting to Narnia, either. Dad says it's because Mum bought it at IKEA." I love the idea that Swedish people are deliberately making non-magical furniture. How very wicked of them.

To get back to bookshop pets, we didn't have one of those at Ripping Yarns, though we accidentally came close to adopting one. Imogen, an eight-year-old girl who visited us once a month to spend her pocket money on boarding-school novels, was browsing the shelves one evening with her father. They'd been in the shop about half an hour before I heard her say: "Dad, where's Henry?" I'll admit, I looked up in alarm, thinking Henry was her younger brother, wondering how on earth they could have spent thirty minutes in the shop without realizing he wasn't there. However, it turned out that Henry was not her brother. Henry was her hamster. Her tiny, winter-white dwarf hamster who had been tucked inside her pocket and who, it transpired, had decided to wander off to investigate the bookshop on his own. While on the one hand thinking this would be a great idea for a children's book, and on the other panicking I was about to step on a tiny rodent, I joined them in searching high and low for furry Henry. He wasn't in the sports section. He wasn't reading the crime novels. He wasn't even perusing the cookbook shelves hunting for a snack. After a fraught twenty minutes peering behind every dusty title we could reach, we were able to breathe a sigh of relief. It turned out Henry hadn't made a bid for freedom after all. He'd nibbled at the lining of Imogen's coat pocket and burrowed deep inside it, and there he remained, fast asleep, oblivious to the chaos he'd caused.

Running a bookshop is not always quite so exhilarating. Once, a man vomited on my shoes, for example, but there are many moments I will always remember fondly. Being an antiquarian bookshop—meaning we stocked very old books, not books about fish, which was an oddly common misconception—I had the pleasure of reuniting people with favorite books from their pasts. "The cover was blue," they would say (why it was always blue, I'll never know), or "there were drawings of frogs on the endpapers," or "I think it had the word 'prince' in the title." Often, the book would turn out to be green, they were flowers not frogs, and the word "prince" didn't appear anywhere, but the tracking down of memories was something very special indeed. One day, I received a phone call from a woman who had been looking at our online inventory. She'd spied a collection of nature tales she'd had as a young girl, and her mother had sold it without her permission at a rummage sale decades ago. Now she wanted to buy a copy for her grandchildren. She paid for it over the phone, and I mailed the book to her. The next day, she called me in tears, saying the book I'd sent her was her copy. It had the inscription in the front from her great aunt, and a dent in the corner from where she'd dropped it down the stairs when she was seven. She hadn't seen the book in forty years. Our bookshop was two hundred miles away from her house. She'd heard about us by chance when I'd spoken about books on Radio 4, and then browsed our website on her lunch break. Now she was holding part of her childhood in her hands. It was a surreal, beautiful moment.

As well as working as a bookseller, I write books—and sometimes I write books about bookshops—so, consequently, I have talked to booksellers all around the world, I have travelled to hundreds of bookshops to do events, and I have fallen in love with many of them. (The bookshops, not the booksellers, though it's a close call.) →

I HAVE TRAVELLED TO HUNDREDS OF BOOKSHOPS TO DO EVENTS, AND I HAVE FALLEN IN LOVE WITH MANY OF THEM.

45

RUNNING A BOOKSHOP IS A CURIOUS PROFESSION. IT IS A DELIGHTFUL, WEIRD, AND WONDERFUL THING. I AM GRATEFUL TO HAVE BEEN PART OF IT.

→ I have a particular fondness for traveling bookshops. There's something magical about a bookshop or library that appears and then disappears again. A friend of mine, Sarah Henshaw, runs The Book Barge, a bookshop on a narrowboat complete with a bookshop bunny called Napoleon Bunnyparte. Initially stationed in the UK, now she's based in France, and she has renamed the shop Le Book Barge. In Tehran, if you hail a taxi, you might be picked up by the Ketabraneh, a bookshop inside a taxi run by husband-and-wife team Mehdi Yazdany and Sarvenaz Heraner. Mehdi drives while Sarvenaz asks the passengers what they like to read, pulling out books from between the seats, pockets on the doors, the dashboard, and racks hanging on the windows. When you pay your fare, you can buy a book at the same time. And in the village of Serang on Java, Indonesia, near the country's most active volcanoes, Ridwan Sururi takes books from village to village on the back of Luna, a wild pony he has tamed. His aim is to help the locals learn how to read, and he calls this project Kudapustaka: The Horse Library.

Book Towns are another favorite of mine. You can find them dotted around the world. These are villages that have lost their main industry—where inhabitants have come together and decided to turn parts of their houses, barns, and abandoned buildings into bookshops. Thus, clusters of warm-lit, book-filled rooms sprout up along the main street, making their village a sought-after destination for book lovers everywhere: bookshop tourism. Wigtown, Scotland, has dozens of bookshops, including ReadingLasses, a bookshop-café where you can get married in amongst the bookshelves, as the owner is a humanist celebrant. Fjærland, Norway, is a Book Town on Europe's largest mainland glacier, where workers transport books across six feet of snow on kick-sleds. Jinbocho in Tokyo, Japan, has over seventy bookshops, many of them stacked on the outside of buildings, not too far from pop-up bookshops by NumaBooks x NAM, an arts collective that occasionally creates bookshops in the shape of animals. Because, why not?

Running a bookshop is a curious profession. To be a bookseller is to be a travel guide. To hold the door open to magical places, to hand out maps and guidebooks and the occasional torchlight, too. It is a delightful, stressful, weird, and wonderful thing. I am grateful to have been part of it.

JEN CAMPBELL is a bestselling author and award-winning poet. Her non-fiction titles include The Bookshop Book *and the* Weird Things Customers Say in Bookshops *series.* *www.jen-campbell.co.uk*

BALDWIN'S BOOK BARN

WEST CHESTER · PENNSYLVANIA · USA

Bibliophiles from all over the world have been making the pilgrimage to this enchanted book barn in Pennsylvania for generations

Baldwin's Book Barn lies in a picturesque setting in the heart of the dreamy Brandywine Valley in Pennsylvania. Some 300,000 used and rare books, maps, wonderful collectibles, and art prints fill the five floors of the former barn. William and Lilla Baldwin started running a little secondhand bookstore in nearby Wilmington, Delaware, in 1934.

Twelve years later, in 1946, they and their entire family moved to the historic farm, where they converted the former milking shed into a unique family residence, and transformed the barn into a bookstore. The couple also ran a small local history museum here for a few years. Nowadays, Baldwin's Book Barn counts itself among the best secret insider tips in Chester County. Throughout the summer, the grand old trees bloom all around the farmstead, transforming the book barn into a beautiful, cool retreat. In the winter, a welcoming fire crackles in the rustic old wood oven, warming the many book-lined aisles. Every square inch of these stone walls breathes American history—just like the books that sit excitedly awaiting their new owners. 📖

TOP 300,000 secondhand books await new readers here.

OPPOSITE Baldwin's Book Barn is surrounded by old trees. The owners once ran a little museum of local history here for a few years.

TOP Watch out for the cat! Books and visiting pets coexist in the old barn.

LEFT The structure of the former farmyard building remains beautifully visible to this day.

OPPOSITE Baldwin's Book Barn is one of the loveliest and quirkiest off-the-radar sights in Chester County.

BART'S BOOKS

OJAI · CALIFORNIA · USA

How lots of books and a kind gesture
became the most popular open-air
bookstore in the USA

The history of this bookstore is at least as charming as its sunny Californian setting. Richard "Bart" Bartinsdale had always been an enthusiastic collector of books. When his collection grew too big for him in the early 1960s, he assembled a few bookshelves on the street without further ado and filled them with the excess books. Instead of a cash register, Bartinsdale used a couple of old coffee tins, which he placed on the shelves. Visitors who found a book would just put the right amount in a tin. It's not quite like that today, but Bart's Books has since become probably the most popular open-air bookstore in the USA. Countless local residents and tourists flock to the charming outdoor establishment on the corner of West Matilija Street and Canada Street in Ojai. It is thought that around a million books have passed through Bartinsdale's hands, from small paperbacks for 35 cents to rare first editions and art books valued at several thousand dollars. Today, Matt Henriksen runs Bart's Books as its general manager. Like Bartinsdale, his is also a consummate book lover. "Books are ideas and ideals. →

TOP What started off as a couple of shelves full of antiquarian books is now one of the largest open-air bookstores in the United States.

OPPOSITE Palm trees, blazing sunshine, and books—all you need for a perfect afternoon.

TOP An estimated one million books lie behind the green-swathed façade on the corner of West Matilija Street and Canada Street.

OPPOSITE Those who buy from Bart's Books just throw the right amount into the coffee cans provided.

→ They are the contents of the collected and recorded human experience," he says. Henriksen is completely impartial when putting together the selection of titles. He gives pulp novels the same consideration as poetry and philosophy.

Antiquarian books, new publications, and tattered paperbacks line the labyrinthine aisles of Bart's Books. "Getting the opportunity to facilitate someone else's connection to a life-changing idea is a rare privilege," says the bookseller. "A customer who I knew as a burgeoning actor disappeared for a while. When she showed up again a year later, she told me that a book of poetry I'd recommended had changed her life, and she had been traveling the West Coast reading her poetry. She was a poet now. What an awesome responsibility." 📖

SCARTHIN BOOKS

CROMFORD · UNITED KINGDOM

This tucked-away bookstore has been going strong for over 40 years thanks to a loyal customer base and a wonderfully experienced team

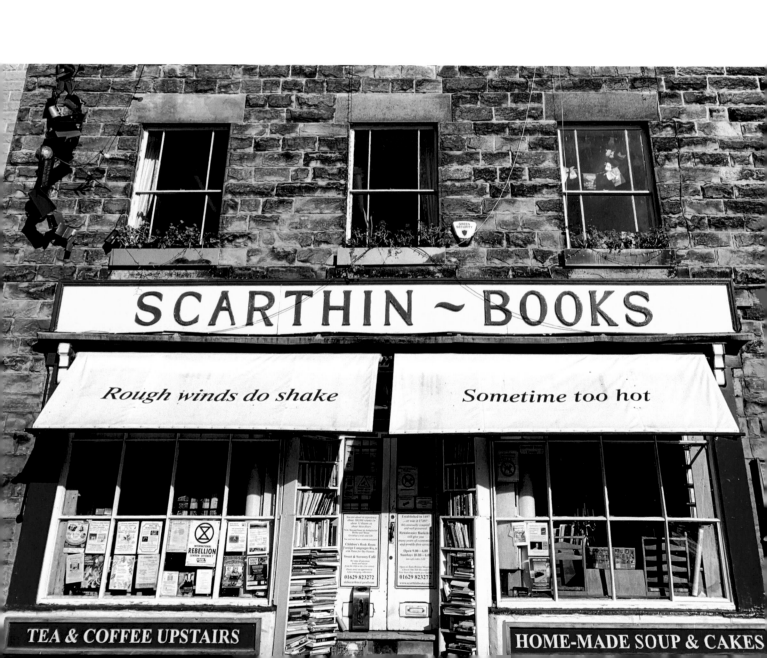

S carthin Books isn't the type of bookstore that you just stumble upon. Those perusing the bookshelves have made their way to this little waterside promenade in the village of Cromford quite deliberately. "That's something we really appreciate," says David Booker, who runs the carefully arranged store. Scarthin Books is owned by Dave Mitchell, who set it up in his own house in the 1970s and is now retired. Mitchell says that Scarthin is "a sort of museum that visitors are allowed to buy a little piece of." And its loyal crowd of regulars do just that; indeed, they love this cozy bookstore so much that they once financed renovations to the building via a crowdfunding campaign. "We are not perfect, far from it. When books are coming through our doors at an alarming rate (which is often), we can be more than a little untidy, and finding what you are after can sometimes feel like something of a quest, but we try our very best." The fact that sales are increasing despite the store's obscure location proves that Booker is getting it right. The comfy armchair in the Art Room is almost always occupied, and the program of events generates huge interest. The vegetarian café is also a big hit, enthuses Booker. "Have a natter over a cuppa and a slice of cake," he says—"what could be nicer?" 📖

57

FLOATING THE BOOK LOVER'S BOAT

THE BOOK BARGE · CANAL DU NIVERNAIS · FRANCE

Escape and go on a journey with a book. This floating bookstore sells its valuable cargo all along the canal—and 100 percent offline

The Book Barge is going against the current—or, more precisely, against the Amazonian current, stresses Sarah Henshaw with a wink. And she means it literally: her floating bookstore is the opposite of the online giant in almost every respect. "In 2011...when a lot of other independent bookshops were being forced to close down because of the aggressive discounting of online and chain stores, I took the boat on an experimental six-month tour of the UK's inland waterways, trying to get people to re-evaluate a book's worth," says the bookseller. At that point, the Book Barge was completely unsuitable as a place to live, as there was no bathroom, kitchen, or bed on board the charming, book-filled vessel.

As she went along, Henshaw therefore bartered her literary freight for food and lodging: "The latest hardback for a home-cooked dinner, or a stack of secondhand children's encyclopedias for a spare sofa to sleep on that night," she recalls. "For a few heady weeks in London, I was even able to write out lengthy shopping lists, hand them to a customer, and swap books to the value of the till receipt and bagged groceries they returned later that day. As well as being a useful corrective to the easy acceptance that value for money has just one currency, the trip was transformative in other ways, too. Not least because it taught me that books are gateways to new friendships and experiences—not just within their pages, but by the simple act of being passed along to the next reader."

Of course, there is a certain order to the selection of titles on the Book Barge. The books are roughly arranged into adult and children's literature. In any case, Henshaw knows exactly where every book is and is happy when customers →

59

I TOOK THE BOAT ON AN EXPERIMENTAL SIX-MONTH TOUR, TRYING TO GET PEOPLE TO REEVALUATE A BOOK'S WORTH.

TOP The boat's kitchen also serves as a cozy reading nook for delighted visitors.

LEFT The selection of titles in the Book Barge is changing constantly and may also serve as a means of payment for food and accommodation.

OPPOSITE Wild at heart: Sarah Henshaw is constantly steering her 60-foot-long book boat onward to new shores and new adventures. And having her own bookstore means doing it in style.

→ simply draw inspiration from the range and allow themselves to chance upon something unexpected. "When I used to live on the boat, customers were always in danger of finding laundry or other embarrassing personal items shoved behind the spines," says Henshaw. "That sometimes added a certain frisson, for sure!"

In June 2016, she boated across the English Channel to Calais, ending up in Bordeaux, where the store currently operates. "I am the master of my fate/I am the captain of my soul," she says, quoting the poet William Ernest Henley. "That's pretty much how it feels to be at the helm of a 60-foot floating bookstore. Those lines reflect something of the indomitability I still get standing there." 📖

61

TOP Having your own bookstore
is the ultimate in style.

BÓKIN

REYKJAVÍK · ICELAND

On the island of fire and ice, a small secondhand bookstore serves as a cultural ambassador for Iceland

Glimpsing the *Edda,* a collection of traditional sagas, and a copy of *In the Land of the Great Snow Bear: A Tale of Love and Heroism,* by adventurer William Gordon Stables, through the frost patterns on the display window—these are sure signs that we're in Iceland. Bókin has been selling everything from classic literature to rare antiquarian books from this store on the outskirts of Reykjavík since 1964. In addition to its loyal band of customers, this little secondhand bookstore primarily supplies libraries and museums in Iceland and abroad. Musicians, artists, and fashion designers are also among the store's fans, and they love browsing the packed shelves or using the cozy aisles for photo shoots. Following several changes of ownership, Ari Gísli Bragason is now the store's happy proprietor. Eiríkur Ágúst Guðjónsson is one of his loyal employees. "Our store is actually constantly changing," he says. Just as well: that's exactly what makes it so wonderful. 📖

RIGHT Iceland expert Eiríkur Ágúst Guðjónsson has worked in the charming bookstore for years.

OPPOSITE Although it appears unlikely at first glance, the team knows the precise location of every book.

65

BACK OF BEYOND BOOKS

MOAB · UTAH · USA

In the middle of the desert lies a small bookstore, the legacy of a writer and environmental activist

"Even in this digital age, the analog book remains the PERFECT technology," says Shari Zollinger, the events manager at Back of Beyond Books. "The book is our link to the history of civilization and the great thinkers of the world." The little bookstore in the Moab desert has been running for over 30 years.

The selection is primarily devoted to books on local topics. Regional nature guides and publications about the environment, North American history, and archaeology have gained it a loyal clientele. "Of course we'll order a romance title, but we're decidedly unromantic in our genre selections," says Zollinger.

The history of Back of Beyond is particularly intriguing: the bookstore is an homage to the desert and the U.S. writer and wilderness expert Edward Abbey, who wrote about an alliance of environmental activists struggling against the destruction of their beloved natural world in his novel *The Monkey Wrench Gang*. The gang's hiding place, in the middle of nowhere, was called the Back of Beyond. 📕

HONESTY BOOKSHOP

HAY-ON-WYE · UNITED KINGDOM

My kingdom for a book—how the owner of a castle made his dream of an honesty bookstore come true—and in doing so created a whole book town

TOP Everything starts with an idea: today the little village of Hay-on-Wye is home to some 30 bookstores and hosts a literary festival.

OPPOSITE "King Richard Cœur de Livre" reigns over his realm of books from his castle, only part of which remains habitable.

Not only did Richard Booth have an idea, he also had a plan. The self-styled King Richard Cœur de Livre—which translates roughly as "King Richard Book-Heart"—wasn't satisfied with one bookstore. He wanted a whole town of them! From his residence, the crumbling castle that overlooks the Welsh village of Hay-on-Wye, he spent the 1960s and 1970s buying countless books from libraries that were closing all over the world, and promptly opened up several bookstores within stores in the little town that had been standing empty. When he could no longer find room for certain books, Booth opened an honesty bookstore in the castle grounds, which remains hugely popular to this day. Those who find something to read at that store just throw the right amount of change into a box provided for that purpose. Today, Booth's estate is managed by the Hay Castle Trust. Volunteers look after the bookstore, which is open all year round, its shelves protected from the elements only by a makeshift roof. The proceeds from the honesty box go towards maintaining Hay-on-Wye Castle. And Booth's legacy extends far beyond that: many other bookstores have opened in Hay-on-Wye since the 1970s.

The village now boasts around 30 bookstores, despite having a mere 2,000 inhabitants. One story still making the rounds tells of Booth's horse, which the charming eccentric named Prime Minister. The Hay Festival of Literature and the Arts takes place here over ten days every year and now draws in 250,000 visitors. Long live King Book-Heart! 📖

69

HONESTY BOOKSHOP

TOP Richard Booth without his crown: the self-appointed King Book-Heart, who died in 2019, had a unique sense of humor.

LEFT From the very start, this bookstore has operated according to a principle of trust: payment is just thrown into a box.

OPPOSITE People have been wandering around looking for treasures outdoors since back in the 1970s; today, the estate is administered by the Hay Castle Trust.

A feeling for books: volunteer helpers have been ensuring the continued existence of the Honesty Bookshop for years.

REVOLUTIONARY RIGHT FROM THE START

MOE'S BOOKS · BERKELEY · CALIFORNIA · USA

The free-speech movement, anti-war demonstrations, and student protests: this bookstore has seen them all

When Moe and Barbara Moskowitz founded their bookstore together in 1959, these two free spirits very much had their fingers on the pulse. The university town of Berkeley was blossoming under the influence of the Beatniks and the nascent hippie movement when Moe's Books set up just four blocks from the campus of the University of California. A couple of years later, the popular bookstore moved to Telegraph Avenue—a symbol of the counterculture and protest movements of the 1960s and 1970s, and a site that brought Berkeley renown well beyond the United States. Moe's Books has lived through, documented, and helped to shape six eventful decades in the town.

Today, Doris Moskowitz is continuing her parents' legacy, having inherited both their bookstore and their deep affection for books. "My personal affinity for the book as an object and reading as an activity has always been with me," says the bookseller. "My parents started Moe's Books →

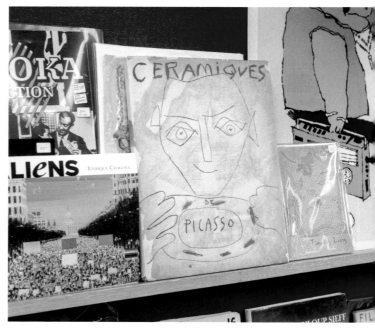

TOP The 200,000-strong selection of titles ranges from political publications to comics and art books.

OPPOSITE The red-and-white striped awning of Moe's Books has long adorned the store's façade on Telegraph Avenue, Berkeley.

MOE'S BOOKS

→ before I was born, and I grew up understanding what it takes to keep it going. Just as we are all driven to keep our homes and gardens the way that we would like them to be, I am driven on a cellular level to make Moe's as beautiful, interesting, easy to use, logical, and cool as possible. This drive is with me every day." The students and countless regular customers who frequent the large bookstore, which has over 200,000 constantly changing titles, know and feel this passion. Moe's Books celebrated its 60-year existence in 2019—with a massive party, of course. Moskowitz knows that books can change lives. "I guess we are in the book business to make both friends and strangers happy. The world we have created is one in which people with open minds can find new ideas and experiences to inspire and delight them." She and her team pour plenty of enthusiasm into putting together an abidingly eclectic program of events, featuring popular readings that see fellow booksellers like Lawrence Ferlinghetti of City Lights →

I GUESS WE ARE IN THE BOOK BUSINESS TO MAKE BOTH FRIENDS AND STRANGERS HAPPY.

TOP Consummate book lover Doris Moskowitz took over the legendary bookstore from her father.

LEFT Moskowitz grew up among books and today enhances the lives of readers with knowledgeable recommendations.

OPPOSITE The range of titles at Moe's Books always reflects the current zeitgeist.

LEFT Free spirit Moe Moskowitz and his bookstore witnessed the hippie counterculture and the free-speech movement.

OPPOSITE TOP The chaotic appearance is deceptive: Moskowitz and her team know exactly which book is hidden in which stack.

OPPOSITE BOTTOM LEFT The store's founder, Moe Moskowitz, died in 1997, but continues to watch over it in the form of the humorous "Almost Moe" bust.

OPPOSITE BOTTOM RIGHT With titles that run the gamut from charming to challenging, Moe's Books is always looking to inspire.

IN AN ENVIRONMENT WHERE ONLY THE CHAIN STORES SEEM TO SURVIVE, MOE'S CONTINUES TO GROW AND FLOURISH.

→ or bestselling writers like Dave Eggers take to the stage or simply attend as part of the audience. Should the fancy take the team, new launches might be celebrated with a midnight release party. One example was the legendary party to mark the launch of Thomas Pynchon's *Against the Day,* with themed music and drinks. In Moe's bookstore, through Moskowitz's curatorship, the free spirit of the 1960s survives alongside a drive to be accessible and relevant today, keeping its vibrant heritage alive. "In an environment where only the chain stores seem to survive, Moe's continues to grow and flourish," says Moskowitz. "My hope is that there will always be room in the world for independent, locally owned, women-owned, family-owned and operated, pet-friendly bookstores like Moe's. Enjoy life, read more books!"

LIBRERIA ACQUA ALTA

VENICE · ITALY

This charming bookstore is one
of the most visited attractions
in Venice

W here but Venice would you find a bookstore that keeps its books, completely unsorted, in old gondolas, bathtubs, and barrels? The entrance to the delightful, yet chaotic, Libreria Acqua Alta lies down a little alleyway about a third of a mile from the Piazza San Marco. The interior is crammed with books—and tourists, who shuffle through the aisles amazed, taking photos, browsing through the towers of books, and gazing out from the little canalside terrace at the back of the building. A staircase built entirely of books leads back to the hustle and bustle of the City of Lagoons. Luigi Frizzo opened the unusual bookstore in 2002. Today, his son Lino runs the business. The location "was big enough to let me bring a lot of books in and let me put different elements of Venice together," Luigi Frizzo said. "Paper and water usually don't fit very well, but they did in this particular place." Five cats purr between the books and allow customers to pet them. Besides their decorative purpose, the gondolas have another, highly practical function: in case of "acqua alta," or high water—i. e., flooding—the books here are safe from harm, at least for a while. 📖

TOP Discarded books are stacked up in the narrow passageway behind the bookstore, where they yellow in the Venetian sun.

BOTTOM The Libreria Acqua Alta lies just a couple of inches above the water level—and sometimes beneath it.

OPPOSITE The bookstore's gondolas have made it famous, with piles of books where the gondolieri normally stand and sing.

LIBRERIA ACQUA ALTA

TOP How apt: discarded books lead the way up a staircase.

LEFT The front entrance of the Libreria Acqua Alta lies tucked away near Venice's famous Piazza San Marco.

OPPOSITE Those who seek shall find ... a new favorite read might just be hiding in one of the old bathtubs.

STRAND BOOKSTORE

NEW YORK CITY · USA

This almost 100-year-old bookstore is the American Dream come true

LEFT Nancy Bass Wyden is in the third generation of the family running the Strand Bookstore. She took over the store from her father, Fred Bass.

BOTTOM New Yorkers love stopping off here: this little outpost of the bookstore has a superb selection of literature.

OPPOSITE The Strand Bookstore has been a landmark on New York's Broadway for over 50 years. It was previously located on Book Row in Greenwich Village.

New York just wouldn't be New York without the Strand Bookstore. Located on Broadway, the iconic store now covers a remarkable 54,000 square feet, offers books on every conceivable topic, and has served over 2.5 million customers. It is hard to believe that this empire was founded almost a century ago by a 26-year-old with a three-hundred-dollar loan. Benjamin Bass started his business in 1927 in the Greenwich Village district of New York. His son Fred grew up among the books and was helping his dad out in the store by the time he was a teenager. Together, they scoured New York for books. In the late 1950s, the Strand Bookstore moved to the corner of Broadway and 12th Street, where it remains to this day. Fred's daughter Nancy now successfully manages the family business and has expanded Strand's wares to offer quirky literary accessories—from a mug with Shakespearean insults to the popular Strand Books romper suit— not to mention a packed program of events that draws in regulars, tourists, and celebrities like rock legend Patti Smith. 📖

TOP The heavy leather arm-chairs create a little reading island that is a coveted spot for many of the regulars.

LEFT There's always room for a bit of dry humor among the shelves of the Strand Bookstore.

OPPOSITE New Yorkers have been indulging their taste for good literature here for almost 100 years.

CULTIVATING COMMUNITY

Why a good bookstore offers so much more than what's on the shelves

Few places bring hope to the soul like a bookstore. Within the rows of neatly stacked titles lies the possibility of transformation, the opportunity of being gripped so tightly by a story—real or imagined—that it changes forever the way we view the world. While reading itself may be an act we perform (mostly) in solitude, the stories we uncover and the knowledge we gain from books is something we feel compelled to debate, discuss, and dissect—even with strangers. The genesis of those heartfelt conversations often begins within the walls of a bookstore, when we are drawn toward the idea that the next right book is just moments away from entering our lives. The role of the bookstore owner has long been to assist us in this journey from wanting to having. Countless tales are relayed every day of bookstore owners who have an uncanny ability to understand people's needs (even those they never speak of) and find a book to meet them. There are bookstore owners who understand that the experience they're creating is so much more than sharing physical items for sale, and they are the ones who have been able to cultivate communities that stay loyal to their stores, regardless of cheaper, faster, or closer alternatives." But how? By creating experiences that offer the opportunity for genuine connection between the bookstore and its audience. Key to building those experiences is knowing who your audience actually is. What do they most long for from a bookstore? Why are they visiting it? How can you best uncover, then serve, their needs? Community can only result when you first know your audience's needs and wants and then are able to meet (or exceed) these.

For Happy Valley bookstore owner Chris Crouch, knowledge of his audience resulted from being a member of it himself. Located in Collingwood, an inner suburb of Melbourne, Australia, Happy Valley is known for its impeccably curated collection of stunning books, ranging from design and decor to food and fashion. While the bulk of the store is devoted to books, Happy Valley also sells gifts produced by local designers and makers. As a resident of Collingwood for more than two decades, Chris understood what the local community wanted from a bookstore. He has been able to tie in Happy Valley events and activations with local businesses, including The Design Files and The Cancer Council. Such events not only strengthen Happy Valley's bond with its local community, but enable a wider audience to learn about the bookstore's offerings and, in turn, potentially become customers. In addition to running in-store events, Chris also believes that simply working in the store and initiating conversations with customers on a daily basis aids in cultivating community. "I think you have to work in your store, talk to people, and get to know your customer's needs and wants," he says. "From that, your community will grow." One exercise that can aid in uncovering what your audience really wants is to consider what piques their curiosity. What's important to them? What do they believe and value? What type of event or activation would pique their curiosity and ensure that they attend? Are they new moms wanting to learn from parenting experts? Are they first-time homebuyers eager to attend an in-store workshop on budgeting? Are they designers looking to understand their craft on a deeper level? How might you not only offer books that speak to these needs, but offer experiences that do as well? How might your physical space pique their curiosity?

"When we started out, we had a clear objective that we wanted to create a community space that had a retail aspect to it," says artist Maggie May. She and her partner, musician Josh Kelly, run Think Thornbury, a bookstore, workshop venue, and creative space in Thornbury (Melbourne, Australia). "We decided to call it 'Think Thornbury,' as we wanted the space to encourage thought around our interactions with consumable products, and Thornbury to make it clear that we were here for the local community." Since launching in 2017, the couple have offered an array of community-building, curiosity-piquing experiences for their Thinkers, including local music nights, clothing exchanges, public talks, and wellness and meditation events. Bookstore owners, says Maggie May, should consider "the difference between a 'shop' and a 'community-focused shop.' The former follows a traditional business model, while the latter goes a little deeper into fostering a community. There are several different aspects to this. Firstly, what is your business's role within your local community? If you are a bookstore, then your role might be to provide thoughtful gifts to the community and to spread and nurture ideas. Secondly, you must think about your suppliers. If you aren't going to champion suppliers from your local community, then who will? Finally, what can you do with your premises that goes beyond selling products? What type of events or talks can you host? Can you run a fundraiser? Can you offer a space to support people in your community who struggle with mental health or another important issue?"

Maggie May is quick to point out that the duo had no marketing budget when they began. They utilized the word-of-mouth promotion that results from successful in-store experiences to help propel their business forward. They published their events by talking with other locally minded businesses, collaborating with local makers and showing up regularly on social media. "Slowly but surely, the word got out, and we have now arrived at a point where we have a real community around us."

While an instant community is a nice ideal, the reality for most bookstore owners is that being able to achieve one only comes with time. Readings, one of the most iconic bookstores in Australia with seven locations across the country, has been working on nurturing its community since its doors first opened in Carlton in 1969. In doing so, it has consistently found new ways to connect with and engage its audience. "I think the best idea we have implemented to build community, was, and continues to be, our events program," says Mark Rubbo, the managing director. "When we began it in 1985, we were the only bookstore in the country doing it. Having a regular events program meant that we

had to communicate it, and that meant we had to start a magazine to publicize it; if we had a magazine, we had to develop a mailing list; as postage costs went up, a website and social media was a cost-effective way of reaching more people. Of course, most good bookstores now have event programs, so it doesn't seem that original, but it is effective in bringing people together and building community."

From these live events to allowing locals to advertise rooms for rent, jobs, and events on its store's side windows, Readings has always been community-led—a trait that allowed them to withstand the giant American bookstore chain Borders opening (and eventually closing) across the road from their main location, as well as to weather the eCommerce storm fueled by online-only retailers. In addition to investing in researching their audience through surveys and online analytics, Readings also chose to set themselves apart not by price, but by experiences. Today, through surveys and online analytics, Readings also chose to set themselves apart not by price, but by experiences. Today, it runs close to 400 events per year. "I don't see Readings as just a retailer," says Rubbo. "My advice to others would be: be different and do →

LEFT Maggie May and Joshua Kelly also host creative workshops at their bookstore, Think Thornbury.

FOLLOWING PAGE TOP LEFT Think Thornbury focuses on supporting local artists.

FOLLOWING PAGE TOP RIGHT AND BOTTOM Happy Valley is a blend of bookstore and record store, and you can also buy art prints and small gifts.

MY ADVICE TO OTHERS WOULD BE: BE DIFFERENT AND DO NOT TRY TO BEAT THE COMPETITORS ON PRICE. IF YOU ARE DIFFERENT, YOU WILL BUILD UP A LOYAL CORE.

not try to beat the competitors on price. If you are different, you will build up a loyal core."

Yet, for bookstore owners just starting out, the concept of being different can be daunting. One tactic to aid with this is to consider the different needs your audience has in all stages of the buying cycle (the five stages that most customers will go through when interacting with your brand: awareness, research, evaluation, purchase, and post-purchase and advocacy). One of the best ways to build community around your business is to map your ideal customer's journey from start (hearing about your bookstore) to finish (becoming an ambassador for it). What could you do at various points in the buying cycle to help them engage with your store and attract others to it? An annual fundraising event? A monthly get-together? A weekly literary podcast or Facebook Live stream? Or perhaps your difference will be shown through more staff training and data processes so customers feel you "get" them through customization (offline and online). By mapping the ideal customer journey, you begin to see the points at which community helps both your bookstore and its audience grow.

Another way a bookstore can differ from its competitors is to collaborate with people and brands that strengthen your brand story. "As a shop, stand for something," says Crouch. "Don't be too broad, and stick to your strengths." For Maggie May and Josh Kelly, giving back to their local community is a huge part of their brand story. In early 2020, when Australia

was hit with horrendous bushfires, the duo decided to collaborate with their audience to create an online auction, the proceeds of which were donated to help those impacted by the fires. Using social media to promote this, they were inundated with offers, with more than 150 people donating a product or service. The weekend auction raised more than $19,000 for charity and further strengthened their brand's connection with the community. Likewise, Readings has been able to forge a community by seeking out relevant community-minded collaborators. Rubbo suggests that "the best way to build your community when you're starting is to reach out to local gathering places and organizations: schools, kindergartens, libraries, neighborhood associations, mothers' groups. Offer to publicize what they do or host events for them so that they see you as an important part of their community."

When it comes to building your community, there are no rules. If events don't work for you, consider another channel. If you find yourself loving a new brand, ask how they helped instill that feeling in you and whether that's something you could replicate in your bookstore business. Consider whom you share a like-minded audience with and how you might collaborate to bring together, and grow, both of your communities. "A community needs diversity, so don't look at other shops and copy their offerings," suggests May. "Instead, look for people and brands who are not represented in your area and prioritize them. This means talking to people, visiting

markets, having late-night scrolling adventures on Instagram, and reading blogs. If you interact with your community, you will find gems who need your support. It takes hard work to curate an original offering and your store will be more special and more frequented by your community as a result." Crouch agrees. "The biggest lesson is 'never stand still,'" he says. "Retail needs constant change. Happy Valley reflects the local design community with lots of interesting and thoughtful books, and I only stock things I can get excited about. If I can't get excited about what I do, then how can I expect my customers to get excited?" Ultimately, cultivating community is about cultivating relationships. People may, in time, forget the details of the book they bought from your store, but if the store has been created so as to provide not only products but passion, they will never forget the experience and how your store made them feel.

FIONA KILLACKEY is the founder of My Daily Business Coach, a consultancy that helps creative small business owners with branding, marketing, and business systems. She has written on business, brand, design, and culture for Cool Hunting, Monocle, Refinery29, The Design Files, *and* SOMA, *among other titles.*

HIGH-PROOF LITERATURE

DYSLEXIA LIBROS · ANTIGUA · GUATEMALA

Upon discovering that his bar was located next to a school, the owner promptly transformed the front room into his dream bookstore

RIGHT The owner of Dyslexia Libros has a real weakness for good books and old doors.

OPPOSITE Mixed doubles: international literature to the left, rambunctious live music and mezcal to the right.

John Rexer had always had an inkling that a little bookstore could save the world. He now runs Dyslexia Libros, his dream bookstore, in Antigua. At first, he was only looking to open a mezcal bar, and the front room opened directly onto the street, Rexer explains. When work began, he says, "my landlord came by and said, 'You are directly next door to a school—and it's illegal to have a bar next to a school.' So, after a few drinks, I asked my landlord, 'What do you think if I put a bookstore in front of the bar?' He said, 'Perfect!' So, basically, I have a speakeasy bar sitting behind the bookstore."

Rexer dreamed of having a bookstore stocked with good contemporary and classic literature, plus a selection of books on topics like architecture, archaeology, and history. At the same time, he had no idea how to get his hands on good books in Guatemala. Books in English and other foreign languages were particularly difficult to come by. "But sometimes, when you leave things in the hands of the book gods, surprising things happen," he says.

"One very rainy day in Antigua, my dog was hit by a car. I picked her up in my arms and walked all the way to the other side of town, where I knew there was a veterinary [clinic]. While my dog was being treated, I noticed there were bookshelves on the walls of the clinic. The books were for sale to raise money for animals living in the street. I picked a book off the shelf, and it was a first edition Eugene O'Neill: *Long Day's Journey Into Night.*" Beside it was a first edition of a novel by Anthony Burgess. Trawling through the books on the shelf, Rexer discovered one good book after another; some were paperbacks, others hardcovers. Each book was priced at 10 quetzals—less than $1.50. "When the veterinarian came out with my dog bandaged up, I asked him how often they sold a book. He said, 'About three or four a month.' I asked if he would sell them all right now. And his response was, 'If you count them, I'll sell them.' So, for about four hundred dollars, I bought my first three hundred or so books." And that's not all: it turned out that U.S. writer Gore Vidal had lived in Antigua for a time in the 1940s. These very books had belonged to one of his lovers. Before Vidal died, he had donated the books, each of which contained his dated signature on the first page, to the veterinary clinic.

Today, Rexer shares his passion with a loyal clientele—not to mention those who frequent his mezcal bar. "I see my bookstore as a flypaper →

I WANTED TO HAVE A NAME THAT MADE PEOPLE STOP AND THINK, MAYBE LAUGH, BE INTRIGUED, ASK "IS THIS A BOOKSTORE FOR DYSLEXICS?"

TOP Dyslexia Libros is the bookstore of owner John Rexer's dreams. He only stocks his favorite books.

LEFT In Antigua, the bookstore-plus-bar is a hotspot for creatives and those working in the cultural sector.

OPPOSITE Tom Grenzner, a writer and important figure in the community, reads at the Dyslexia After Dark series of events.

→ for catching interesting people," he says glee-fully. Together with the bar, the name Dyslexia Libros also creates its own pull. "I kind of love the word. Look at it. It's like 'giraffe,' there is some-thing playful about the word. I wanted to have a name that made people stop and think, maybe laugh, be intrigued, ask 'is this a bookstore for dyslexics?' Plus, you should meet the people who work in my bookstore, they are all a bit confused.

"I once told a friend of mine that I think a small bookshop with a great selection of books can save the world. I said, 'It's sort of my messi-anic complex.' And his response to me was, 'You put the messy in messianic.'"

Besides books and interesting words, top-ics of conversation at the bar sometimes include another of Rexer's passions: he collects old doors. "I probably have hundreds of them, some from old homes, some from old farms, different styles. And I see books as [the] same thing, they are col-lections of doors to other worlds." He is so fond of certain books that he lends them out as often

as he can. A special shelf labeled John's Teasers holds titles including *The World of Yesterday* by the Austrian writer Stefan Zweig, Rexer's favorite book. "It reveals [Zweig's] incredible humanity, and decency, and love of intellect, and bravery." Not a lot of people remember him these days, Rexer says, but before Hitler's rise to power, he was one of the most widely read authors in the world. "There is probably no book as relevant to today and the current rise of right-wing govern-ments as *The World of Yesterday.*" Alongside it stands *The God of Small Things* by Indian activist Arundhati Roy and *Small is Beautiful* by British-German economist E. F. Schumacher. "And another thing," laughs Rexer. "If you buy forty quetzals (five dollars) worth of books, we give you a coupon for a free beer in my bar. I'm not sure if I'm trying to encourage reading or drinking." 📖

BOOKS ARE MAGIC

NEW YORK CITY · USA

If you're opening your dream bookstore,
then you're completely free to install a gumball
machine that dispenses poems

"A bookstore is the soul of a neighborhood," says Emma Straub. She and her husband, Michael Fusco-Straub, opened Books Are Magic in 2017, when their favorite bookstore closed. "We knew that we couldn't live in a neighborhood without one, so we picked up the torch. We wanted to open the friendliest bookstore in Brooklyn and serve all of our community's needs, including creating a family-friendly space and hosting lots of literary events to keep the community engaged."

New titles and classics, places for children to hide, and a gumball machine that dispenses wonderful poems instead of chewing gum all await behind the beguiling façade with its pink, hand-lettered "Books Are Magic" sign. With its exposed ceiling beams, bare brick walls and rounded store windows, the bookstore does indeed have a touch of magic about it. "It was exactly what we wanted," enthuses Straub. "If Books Are Magic were a person, she would be smart, funny, and joyous." 📖

TOP Books Are Magic offers wonderful readings and cultural events, along with a specially designed nook for little readers.

LEFT When their favorite bookstore was forced to close, Emma Straub and her husband lost no time in opening their own store.

OPPOSITE The giant pink lettering on the wall of the building has been photographed so often that it has become a minor Instagram celebrity in its own right.

PAPERCUP

BEIRUT · LEBANON

This little store boasts a superb selection
of printed publications and a dedicated
program of cultural events

When Rania Naufal moved back to her native city of Beirut from New York, she already had the idea for Papercup tucked away with her luggage. She opened the little store with its pretty floor tiles in the trendy Mar Mikhaël neighborhood in 2009. "We love what we do," says the enterprising owner. "And we do it with passion." Papercup is devoted to "all things print," she said. It stocks local and international magazines alongside books on art, architecture, design, photography, fashion, and travel. FaR Architects and industrial designer Karim Chaya are the brains behind the linear look of the store. The minimalist interior design provides a pleasing underpinning for the books, showcasing them to perfection. Naufal has added to the concept with a small café, where pretty bistro tables invite visitors to linger over a book, do some work, or simply enjoy a delicious coffee. And that's not all: besides running the store and their own online magazine *The Sounder,* Naufal and her team have enough spare energy to organize regular book readings, signings, and cultural events. 📖

TOP You can do some work over a good coffee, get lost in a book, or have a chat at the little bistro tables at Papercup.

LEFT The Lebanese bookstore focuses on publications about architecture, design, art, fashion, photography, and travel.

OPPOSITE Its mix of tradition and clean modern lines are the work of interior and industrial designer Karim Chaya and FaR Architects.

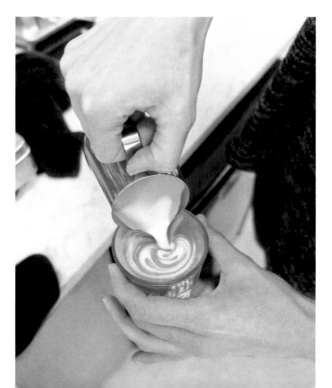

TOP Lebanon is a land of contrasts: the velvety two-seat sofa is set symbolically against a rough backdrop.

LEFT A print product with a difference: the Papercup team serves delicious, freshly brewed coffee.

OPPOSITE The left wall of the bookstore is lined with international and Lebanese magazines focusing on design, architecture, and plenty of other themes.

101

MY HOME IS MY BOOKSTORE

BRAZENHEAD BOOKS · NEW YORK CITY · USA

It was New York's worst-kept secret: a bookseller who had turned his apartment into a bookstore

According to legend, a brazen head is a brass or bronze head that can give a wise answer to any question. Michael Seidenberg, who long ran a supposedly secret bookstore by that very name, did not have a bronze head, but he did have a heart of gold and a book recommendation, at least, for any query. The passionate bookseller became the stuff of legend when, after a hike in rent for his store, he relocated his entire range of books to his own apartment. There, until his death in July 2019, he ran a speakeasy bookstore that could be visited by anyone following a quick registration over the phone. After several moves, Seidenberg's apartment bookstore finally came to rest on the Upper East Side in Manhattan.

Gracie Bialecki, one of Seidenberg's long-time close friends, recalls that "even with bookcases lining every possible wall, there was never enough space for Michael's collection, which overflowed onto tables and teetered in stacks on the floor. On crowded nights, it was often easier to read the titles crowded next to you than do any browsing. There was always something →

TOP Seidenberg regularly invited people to secret and not-so-secret soirées, which visitors still rave about today.

OPPOSITE After being evicted from his first apartment for wrongful use, Seidenberg simply continued at his next address.

BRAZENHEAD BOOKS

→ tucked into the shelves, be it a first edition, a tobacco pipe, or memorabilia from Michael's travels." It is hardly surprising that Seidenberg's remarkable bookstore soon became a secret—or not-so-secret—gathering place for enthusiastic readers, writers, and a glorious variety of New York citizens. This was due in no small part to the fact that Seidenberg himself seemed to have stepped straight out of a novel. He treated his books like good friends and only entrusted them to loving hands. He endorsed books that were particularly dear to him with the inscription "priceless." The Mystery Cabinet contained select curiosities. Seidenberg's favorite writer, John Cowper Powys, whose novel *The Brazen Head* gave the store its

name, was honored with a little shrine. And almost every evening, the store was thronged with people reading and having a good time.

"Michael's salons often ran late into the night," says Bialecki, who remembers those days fondly. "With the curtains drawn and the books covering the windows, time stood still at Brazenhead. Along with the popular salons, there were also open poetry readings, as well as individual appointments for the book lovers Michael always made it a point to accommodate."

"We're thankful for all the years he opened his door and heart to us," Bialecki concludes. Will there ever be another bookstore quite like it? Only the brazen head can say. 📖

THE SALONS OFTEN RAN LATE INTO THE NIGHT WITH THE BOOKS COVERING THE WINDOWS, TIME STOOD STILL.

LEFT AND TOP Personal belongings, travel souvenirs, and little notes were often to be found among the books.

OPPOSITE Seidenberg himself did not know how many characters from novels were sharing his home, but knew the location of every single book by heart.

TOP Seidenberg treated
his books like good friends,
and only entrusted them
to loving hands.

LEFT Brazenhead Books
lived the literary *dolce vita*
almost every night.

OPPOSITE Seidenberg
could enthuse anyone he
met about books.

Golden Hare Books

FINE BOOKS

BOOKS

FOR ADULTS →

CHILDREN

OPENING HOURS
10-6 every day

DOG FRIENDLY!

wifi

GOLDEN HARE BOOKS

EDINBURGH · UNITED KINGDOM

This little store was named Independent Bookshop of the Year at the 2019 British Book Awards

I never dreamed that I could be in a job I love so much," says Julie Danskin, laughing. She is the manager of Golden Hare Books, a small and lovingly curated bookstore in the leafy Edinburgh neighborhood of Stockbridge. Her dedicated team works hard to put together a constantly changing program of events, plan writing workshops, issue the store's own podcast, and put on the Golden Hare Book Festival. Behind the store's royal-blue façade, graphic novels sit alongside young adult fiction, while art books rub shoulders with cookbooks and books about nature. The coziest section of all may well be the little paradise of children's books at the back, where even grown-up readers will love to browse.

The indefatigable owner, Mark Jones, who is currently also on the board of the National Trust for Scotland, is actively involved in shaping the direction of Golden Hare Books. At the same time, he has completely entrusted his vision of a modern bookstore to Julie Danskin and her staff. "Edinburgh is very well-served by indies, and we're delighted to be one of them," says Danskin. She is always on the lookout for special new books for Golden Hare. "Our stock is deliberately kept small—never more than 2,500 titles. It changes all the time, so you never visit the same bookshop twice." Some of the most popular books were stocked following recommendations from customers. The bookstore has won many local fans thanks to its appealing, inclusive program, and that connection goes well beyond a simple business relationship: "We get to see people on first dates, we help people find books appropriate for the happiest and saddest of life's events, and best of all, we get to see children grow up excited about books!"

LEGERE HUMANUM EST! TO READ IS HUMAN!

DESPERATE LITERATURE · MADRID · SPAIN

Literature runs through the very veins
of the young and committed owners
of this lively bookstore

A quote from Joaquín Font, a character from Roberto Bolaño's *The Savage Detectives*, adorns the wall of this small bookstore: "There are books for when you're bored. Plenty of them. There are books for when you're calm. The best kind, in my opinion. There are also books for when you're sad. And there are books for when you're happy. There are books for when you're thirsty for knowledge. And there are books for when you're desperate." Desperate Literature is a joint venture by Terry Craven, Charlotte Delattre, Corey Eastwood, and Craig Walzer, who also runs Atlantis Books on Santorini. The four young founders come from Europe and the United States, and they are now living out their shared dream of a literature-steeped life in Madrid.

This remarkable literary hotspot is now run by Delattre and Craven, who began his bookselling career at Shakespeare and Company in Paris in 2007. "It was something of a revelation to me, the moment I walked through those doors. I was the perfectly starry-eyed young tumbleweed (writer-in-residence) and the life swallowed me up: meeting writers and readers, people falling in love and fighting over literature, rummaging through boxes in search of treasures, unpacking the latest releases. It was heaven and I've wanted to hold on to that ever since. Then, slowly but surely, I began to realize the true potential of running a bookstore, which is almost endless, really: you want to publish books, you can do it; you want to have a dance party at 3 p. m., you can do it; you want to host an art show, you can also do it. I love the thought that we can make this place resemble our literary dreams, and that for some of us this means hunting amazing books, for some it means hosting great events, while for others it's about community. It remains as fresh as you want it to be."

Fresh is an apt description of the concept of Desperate Literature. It is apparent in the Poetry Phone, inspired by the Beat Generation authors; the (now defunct) Boozy Book Section where books came with spirits and cocktails, with a shot of whiskey for every book bought; and events like the weekly readings and the →

LEFT The shelves are stocked with the team's favorite books and recommendations from loyal customers.

OPPOSITE "A store stays as fresh as you want it to be" is one of the tenets of Desperate Literature.

DESPERATE LITERATURE

LEFT "Bookstores have almost endless potential," believes co-owner Terry Craven.

BELOW Paris-born Charlotte Delattre works alongside Craven to keep things running smoothly at Desperate Literature.

OPPOSITE A quote from a beloved literary character gave the store its name; it is inscribed over the aisles.

I LOVE THE THOUGHT THAT WE CAN MAKE THIS PLACE RESEMBLE OUR LITERARY DREAMS.

→ English-language poetry festival. That festival took place for the first time in May 2019 in Madrid, in conjunction with the Spanish initiative Unamuno Author Series, and featured over 60 poets and academics. "It was a bit bonkers, to be honest, but ridiculously beautiful," enthuses Craven, who, along with his team, also established a literary prize for new experimental short stories. This competition is open for submissions every year between November and March and actively promotes the creativity and careers of the winners. An artist's residency at the Civitella Ranieri Foundation, cash prizes, meetings with literary agents, publishing opportunities, and

Europe-wide readings are all up for grabs. "Really, we are also creating a space for people to meet and care for one another," says Craven. "That might mean making them a cup of tea, it might mean offering a place to stay, or it might just be chatting about literature. Or lending our personal copy of *Moomin Valley in November* to a man vying for love," he says. Together with the team's firm favorites, the shelves are also stocked with recommendations from regular →

→ customers. "Desperate Literature is a place of mutual learning, like all good bookshops."

If to read is human, then to live your life in a bookstore must be approaching the divine. And sharing this serendipity as much as they can with their patrons, whether they are regulars after their next literary fix or travelers alighting for just a moment, means a lot to the team.

Craven actually got that borrowed book back, and to him it illustrates how much power books can have. "When your copy of *Moomin Valley in November* is returned to you," he said, "long after you thought it lost to happenstance, and not by the man who borrowed it but by the couple who fell in love over it, well, then you also know what books can mean." 📖

THERE ARE ALSO BOOKS FOR WHEN YOU'RE SAD. AND THERE ARE BOOKS FOR WHEN YOU'RE HAPPY.

TOP The team has launched its own literary award for new experimental short stories.

OPPOSITE In need of inspiration? Browsing the jam-packed shelves of Desperate Literature is bound to help.

BOOK THERAPY

PRAGUE · CZECH REPUBLIC

If you've ever dreamed about spending
the evening alone in a bookstore in Prague,
then you've come to the right place

LEFT One book in, one book out: this system keeps the selection fresh and interesting.

BOTTOM Anyone who feels like it can spend a whole evening alone with the books at Jiri and Petra Caudr's bookstore.

OPPOSITE One of Book Therapy's areas of focus is selected publications on art and design.

No staff, no other customers—just a bottle of good Czech wine, a hand-picked playlist, and hundreds of amazing books: Petra and Jiri Caudr have certainly hit upon a brilliant idea. The owners of Book Therapy regularly rent out their lovingly furnished store to bibliophiles for three hours after closing time. Visitors can peruse the neatly arranged shelves in complete peace. The design-focused selection of titles ranges from brightly colored vegan cookbooks to Monocle guides. All of the books are prominently displayed like little works of art, with their covers facing outwards. "And we do have a strict rule—one new title in means one older going out as the space is really limited and the clarity within a shop is key," explain the owners. Book Therapy also offers the Flowers & Dinosaurs subscription service especially for parents and children. The team works with children's psychologists to pick two particularly good children's books each month, "for parents who want to raise strong and independent personalities."

THREE STYLISH LETTERS

VVG SOMETHING · TAIPEH · TAIWAN

Very, very good: this bookstore lives
and breathes aesthetics as part of an
ambitious overall concept

Just a stone's throw from bustling Zhongxiao East Road lies a little wonderland, almost hidden away and swathed in greenery. VVG Something is the kind of bookstore where visitors are only too happy to get lost. Behind the red door marked 13, the store itself is lined with dark wooden shelves. Although the space is small, one look at the selection of books is enough for visitors to realize that they've stumbled upon a real treasure trove of inspiration. All mixed in together, and in no apparent order, there's an amazing array of illustrated books, reference works, literature from here, there, and everywhere, and paraphernalia from all four corners of the globe, assembled by the team. "Taste is applied aesthetics" is the bookstore's motto. "Our concept is geared towards men and women aged around 30 and over who want to enjoy art and culture but lack a professional background," explains Julian Chin of the VVG Something team. "We select books and magazines by category, such as photography, illustration, films, tourism, home decoration, gardening, design, [and food] from major cities abroad and introduce them to Taiwanese readers."

The team organizes regular small-scale exhibitions and holds art workshops on a wide range of themes, all with that purpose in mind. The bookstore is part of a broader concept that began in 1999 in a Taipei restaurant. "We've just continued with our efforts to bring beauty into →

TOP A small but exquisite literary wonderland lies hidden behind the red door with the number 13.

OPPOSITE The selection is intuitively put together by Julian Chin and his team, without fixed categories.

VVG SOMETHING

LEFT The block capitals aren't just decorative, but are also used in various workshops.

BOTTOM The selection of books at VVG Something consists of new publications, classics, and antiquarian finds.

OPPOSITE The bookstore holds workshops on a number of themes, from printing to creative writing.

VVG SOMETHING DARES TO REPRESENT MINORITIES, AND IN DOING SO, HAS TRIGGERED A TREND OF ITS OWN IN TAIWAN.

→ every detail of everyday life," Chin says. Today VVG includes several restaurants and boutiques, a catering service, the bookstores VVG Something and VVG Thinking, and a bed and breakfast.

The idea of thinking outside the box remains the raison d'être of the team and is reflected in the range of wares on sale at VVG Something. Bizarre and stylish finds from around the world make the bookstore something of an Aladdin's cave. The big table in the middle of the store serves as both an exhibition space and a workshop area. Visitors can leaf through picture books, some of them rare, over a freshly brewed coffee. "Independent bookstores are all about giving readers and customers an active steer and

showing them what lies outside the mainstream," Chin says. "The world will always have a need for the perspectives of minority groups in order to expand our definitions and standards of beauty. VVG Something dares to represent such minorities, and in doing so, has triggered a minor trend of its very own in Taiwan," he concludes. He's clearly not the only one to deem this VVG—very, very good. 📖

MUNDO AZUL

BERLIN · GERMANY

This children's bookstore invites readers on a fascinating journey around the world with original-language books and cross-border cultural projects

Mundo Azul, the name of this children's bookstore in Berlin, reveals the intention behind it: the shelves are stocked with titles from all over the world, from Portugal to Korea—and all in their original language. "I have a vivid memory of a typical day in the store last winter," says the owner, Mariela Nagle, who is from Argentina. "While browsing the shelves, a German man, a lady from the U.S., two women from Saudi Arabia, and a French illustrator got chatting. It was brilliant. Books are great at bringing people together." Mundo Azul started out in 2007 as a meeting place for Spanish and German families. Today, the little store holds intercultural workshops, provides consultancy for festivals, and supports libraries and universities. "I could read the British author Roald Dahl and the French writer and illustrator Tomi Ungerer all day," says Nagle. "By contrast, I often find German children's book authors a bit too didactic. One of the things I like best is showing that children's books can be so much more in terms of fun, art, and—last but not least—literature."

OPPOSITE The ever-changing selection of titles at Mundo Azul is as vibrant and diverse as the languages of the world.

BOTTOM The bookstore started out as a gathering place for families; today it hosts events including popular workshops.

HAPPY VALLEY

MELBOURNE · AUSTRALIA

A former record store owner has created
a real buzz by selling his favorite books
and music from the space below an old
recording studio

TOP Everything that can be bought from here is intended to make the purchaser happy: the bookstore's name is no mere coincidence.

OPPOSITE Pretty, whimsical little trinkets and gifts can be found between the hand-picked books at Happy Valley.

Just a few years back, Smith Street, in the Melbourne neighborhood of Collingwood, was considered a somewhat disreputable part of town. Fast-forward to today, and it is thronged with creative agencies, exclusive boutiques, and fine restaurants. And at the very heart of it all lies Happy Valley, a store selling books and gifts. Together with a diverse selection of books on design, music, social themes, cuisine, and pop culture, owner Chris Crouch also stocks quirky little items like Tupac pins and build-your-own models of the Sydney Opera House—things you don't need, but absolutely have to own. Not for nothing is the store called Happy Valley: "I wanted Happy Valley to be a store full of optimism, a positive space to browse the 'gallery' feel of our shop," explains Crouch.

As a former record store owner, Crouch is keen on both books and music. His selection of vinyl ranges from albums by U.S. folk group Beirut to records by the legendary Austrian producers Kruder & Dorfmeister. Which makes it all the more fitting that the first floor of the store was used as a recording studio for Australian radio plays back in the 1940s. These walls have stories to tell—just like good books. "A book is forever," muses Crouch. "A book can open minds and your world view that no other medium can do. A book can take so many forms, at different times—educational, informative, escapism and pleasure—sometimes all at once!"

READINGS

MELBOURNE · AUSTRALIA

This bookstore and its community
waged war against a Goliath—
and won

LEFT The independent bookstore has held its own against a big chain thanks to its loyal base of customers.

BOTTOM Owner Mark Rubbo was awarded the Medal of the Order of Australia in recognition of his literary endeavors.

OPPOSITE The success of Readings has made it a role model for independent bookstores in Australia.

If you were to open a bookstore in 1969, you would have found yourself in good company: Ross Reading (yes, you read that correctly) opened his bookstore in the year of the first moon landings and the Woodstock music festival. Almost 50 years on, it has become an icon of the independent bookstore scene. Mark Rubbo now runs the show at Readings. He has received accolades for his services as an exceptional book dealer, opened several stores across Australia, and won the 2016 International Bookstore of the Year award at the London Book Fair. Yet his most prized trophy is of a different kind. When an American chain bookstore opened on the other side of the street in the early 2000s, the fate of its little independent counterpart appeared to be sealed. But the competition hadn't reckoned with the book-loving community of Melbourne's Carlton neighborhood: instead of being lured in by giveaway prices, the customers stayed true to Readings, organizing art campaigns and events until the big chain gave up. David had prevailed over Goliath. 📖

AN AMERICAN IN PARIS

SHAKESPEARE & COMPANY · PARIS · FRANCE

This magical bookstore is a legend, a family reunion, and a social utopia rolled into one

The legendary bookstore Shakespeare and Company opened up in the Rue de la Bûcherie, Paris, in 1951. It lies on the bank of the Seine, opposite the majestic Notre Dame Cathedral. U. S.-born George Whitman first launched his bookstore of English-language literature under the name Le Mistral before re-launching it as Shakespeare and Company a good decade later. In doing so, he was taking on a huge legacy: the bookseller Sylvia Beach had hosted stars of the literary world in her store of the same name. James Joyce, Ernest Hemingway, F. Scott Fitzgerald, Gertrude Stein, T. S. Eliot, and Ezra Pound all came and went, until she was forced to close in 1941 due to the Nazi occupation. When Beach named young Whitman's store the "spiritual successor" to her own, he received the instant patronage of her illustrious clientele. Word quickly spread that an American was running a very special bookstore in Paris. Prominent Beat Generation figures such as Allen Ginsberg and William S. Burroughs were soon stopping by, while Anaïs Nin and Henry Miller proved an enchanting presence. Richard Wright, Julio Cortázar, Lawrence Durrell, and James Baldwin were also among the first visitors to the new Shakespeare and Company.

And they didn't just come for the thousands of books. Whitman established what he described as a social utopia at his bookstore. From the very first day, writers, artists, and intellectuals were permitted to sleep at Shakespeare and Company. The small benches between the full shelves transformed into comfortable beds at night. Since then, an estimated 30,000 creatives have spent the night here. In return, every overnight guest helps out in the store for an hour, promises to read a book, and writes a short biography of themselves, just in case they should ever become a famous writer. →

SHAKESPEARE & COMPANY

→ In 2002, Whitman had a particularly special guest. "I initially started working here to spend time and get to know my estranged father," says Sylvia Whitman, the bookseller's only daughter. At the age of 21, she returned to Paris from England to build a relationship with her father, who was already 88 at the time. "He and the bookstore are completely intertwined, so getting to know him ultimately meant spending time working in the bookstore," she said. "From a desire to get to know George, I then fell in love with Paris, books, and the place he created." After the death of George Whitman in December 2011, Sylvia began running Shakespeare and Company with her partner, David Delannet.

The couple has preserved the concept unchanged. Shakespeare and Company still enjoys cult status as a literary gathering place. The dark wooden shelves still stand on the bookstore's tiled floors. Well-thumbed classics, glossy new releases, paperbacks, and hardcovers—all in English—are piled up in boxes and on, next to, and beneath the tables. Chandeliers illuminate the goings-on across the two floors of the magical bookstore. A ladder leads up to the reading rooms, where readers can really get lost in literary treasures old and new. The stray cat Aggie (named for Agatha Christie, as she was found in the crime section) purrs in her favorite armchair on the first floor. "She now gets her own fan mail," →

FROM A DESIRE TO GET TO KNOW GEORGE, I THEN FELL IN LOVE WITH PARIS, BOOKS, AND THE PLACE HE CREATED.

LEFT For decades, writers have been lending a helping hand, and they are allowed to stay in this bookstore for a little while in return.

OPPOSITE Shakespeare and Company is a Paris institution that lies opposite Notre Dame.; it reopened under new management in 1951, having previously closed during World War II.

INDEPENDENT BOOKSHOPS ARE PLACES OF DISCOVERY, OF CONGREGATION, TO GET LOST IN AND WHILE AWAY THE HOURS.

→ laugh Whitman and Delannet. Over the years, the couple has enhanced the bookstore by adding a café, a bigger children's and art section, and a free weekly program of events, at which major contemporary authors such as Zadie Smith, Don DeLillo, and Rachel Cusk are eager to appear. This magical bookstore, steeped in the creative history of twentieth and twenty-first century Europe, where you may rub shoulders with literary giants or fur with famous cats, or buy a volume from the next great wordsmith, shows the power writing has to bring people together.

The pair are continuing George's legacy, says Whitman, "because independent bookshops are more than just buildings in which books are bought and sold. They are places of discovery, of congregation, places to get lost in and while away the hours. They are places to hear authors talk about their work and engage with them about it, to advance and enrich dialogue, to share stories. As long as any of these needs remain—as long, that is, as humans remain humans—independent bookshops will continue to exist." 📖

133

BEING
OF YOUR OWN
LIGHT
THE ASTONISHING
IN DARKNESS
LONELY OR
WHEN YOU ARE
I COULD SHOW YOU
I WISH

INDEPENDENCE DAY

Independent bookstore numbers are growing around the world, but the day-to-day challenges of life as a small bookstore remain tough

For Philip Pullman, the British author of the award-winning His Dark Materials trilogy, independent bookstores are the "lantern-bearers of civilization." For Neil Gaiman, writing in his fantasy novel *American Gods:* "What I say is, a town isn't a town without a bookstore. It may call itself a town, but unless it's got a bookstore, it knows it's not foolin' a soul." Ask any author, and they will praise independent booksellers to the skies; from Italo Calvino in *If on a Winter's Night a Traveler* to Carlos Ruiz Zafón in *The Shadow of the Wind,* some go so far as to immortalize them in fiction. Others put their money where their mouth is, and open their own stores: George R. R. Martin owns Beastly Books in Santa Fe, New Mexico, Judy Blume has a store in Key West, Florida, and Ann Patchett opened Parnassus Books in Nashville, Tennessee, in 2011. But despite the widespread affection in which the shops are held, life isn't easy for an independent. As George Orwell put it in 1936, "a bookstore is one of the few places where you can hang about for a long time without spending any money." Couple that with the swath that online bookselling has cut through its brick-and-mortar competitors, as well as rising rents, and it's not surprising that independents are in a fight for their lives.

Happily, it's one they currently appear to be winning: online shopping might be cheapest and quickest, but the best independents can offer something more, whether that's the specialist knowledge of a store like The Ripped Bodice, the only exclusively romance bookstore in the United States; the sheer beauty of El Ateneo Grand Splendid, a converted old theater in Buenos Aires; the uniqueness of Venice's Libreria Acqua Alta, which displays its books on gondolas; or the literary history of Paris's Shakespeare and Company. In the United Kingdom, the number of independent bookstores reached a high of 1,894 in 1995, but declined every year until 2016, when numbers had more than halved, to 867 stores. Fortunes then began to turn, according to the UK's Booksellers Association, with an increase in numbers every year since, bringing the total at the end of 2019 to 890. In America, the picture is equally positive. This year, for the tenth year in a row, the American Booksellers Association has reported a growth in independent membership, with stores now operating in 2,524 locations. That's up from 1,651 locations in 2009, as independent stores fill the gap left by the demise of Borders. "As a channel, independent bookstore sales are up," says ABA spokesperson Dan Cullen. "Overall book sales across indie bookstores for 2017 increased 2.6%

over 2016, and sales in 2018 increased nearly 5% over 2017. All of this is a result of the fact that indie booksellers remain a resilient and entrepreneurial group—and that independent bookstores offer a unique, and unparalleled, opportunity for the discovery of new authors and great writing."

In Germany, there are approximately 6,000 bookstores, around 90% of which are smaller independents. According to the German book trade association the Börsenverein des Deutschen Buchhandels, this number hasn't changed significantly over the last five years. In France, the French book trade association the Syndicat de la librairie française says the number of bookstores with at least one employee has remained "practically stable" over the last decade, with 2,344 stores in 2007 and 2,244 in 2017, a decline of 4%. But the SLF says that there are an additional 1,000 bookstores run by just one member of staff. "With more than 3,200 bookstores, France can be proud to have one of the densest networks in the world," said a spokesperson. Both Germany and France enforce fixed prices for books, which puts paid to the wildly competitive cover-price discounting that occurs in the United States and the United Kingdom, putting bricks-and-mortar booksellers at a painful disadvantage to online retailers.

The effects are particularly clear in the UK, where the Net Book Agreement was killed off in the mid-1990s—the exact point at which independent numbers began to drop.

But the positive headline figures belie the challenges independent booksellers are facing every day to survive. As Meryl Halls, chief executive of the UK's Booksellers Association (BA) put it, the small growth in numbers in the United Kingdom is "testament to the creativity, passion, and hard work of our booksellers, who continue to excel in the face of challenging circumstances." But the growth needs to be put in context of "online competition and unequal business rates, all against a backdrop of uncertainty around Brexit and the economy." At Kennys Bookshop in Galway, which was opened in 1940 by Des and Maureen Kenny and which also boasts an art gallery, staff are definitely feeling the pinch of Brexit. "We saw a huge dip in orders from the UK the day after the referendum, and they have not yet recovered," says Sarah Kenny. "The majority of new book releases are published in and supplied from the UK—the delivery times from couriers will likely be longer, which will impact our service massively."

Most booksellers don't own their own property, so will experience upwards-only rent changes—rents are booming everywhere from Berlin to New York. In the United States, one independent bookseller, Michael Seidenberg, saved money by running his legendary appointment-only store, Brazenhead Books, from his apartment on the Upper East Side, until his death in 2019. In London, the owner of Words on the Water, Paddy Screech, gets around ground rent by operating his bookstore from a 100-year-old Dutch barge. But another London store, Camden Lock Books, closed last year, with its owner laying the blame partly at the feet of rising rents. And in New York in 2018, the 100-year-old Drama Book Shop announced its closure thanks to skyrocketing rents. That story at least has a happy ending: Hamilton creator Lin Manuel Miranda stepped in, along with two colleagues, to buy it. Business rates—that is, commercial property taxes—are also a "huge issue" for stores, says Halls. The BA is campaigning for the British government to reform its rates system, which the BA says is "built for an analog age and no longer fit for purpose in our digital and omni-channel era."

"We're always trying to balance up the hard situation it is to be any small business on the high street, and also the fact that for bookstores there is this slight sense of resurgence," says Halls. "There's a growing sense of confidence, with quite a lot of new entrants coming in, but the challenges remain the same. Rent and rates remain the biggest one." Halls highlights the horrors of business rates with the case of BrOOKS, a store in London that found itself slapped with a £11,000-odd business rates bill after a new valuation from Harrow Council. "They took it out of their bank account, →

LEFT Bea and Leah Koch specialize in love stories at their bookstore, The Ripped Bodice.

FOLLOWING PAGE TOP LEFT Michael Seidenberg's Brazenhead Books was a New York institution.

FOLLOWING PAGE TOP RIGHT The Libreria Acqua Alta is one of Venice's many tourist attractions.

FOLLOWING PAGE BOTTOM: Shakespeare and Company in Paris is one of the most famous independent bookstores in the world.

A TOWN ISN'T A TOWN WITHOUT A BOOKSTORE. IT MAY CALL ITSELF A TOWN, BUT UNLESS IT'S GOT A BOOKSTORE, IT KNOWS IT'S NOT FOOLIN' A SOUL.

→leaving them in a situation where they just thought they had to close," says Halls. "They spent months fighting this and have quite recently won their appeal, but it could easily have put them out of business. That's the sort of thing independents are battling. For an independent, certainly in the first three years, they're not making money. Their margins thereafter are tiny, three to four percent, and that's for an established shop. Those external occupancy costs are massive." It used to be the fact that independent booksellers felt their market share was being decimated by the book chains. In the UK and Ireland, this is no longer the case, with the two sectors existing in (relative) harmony. "The big divide is between the high street and online," says Halls. "I think those battle lines are drawn, and independents identify with [the chains,] Waterstones and Blackwell's. Indies do get irritated with Waterstones, but from our point of view, everyone knows the ecosystem needs all of them to be successful. We're delighted to see Waterstones with strong leadership, opening new branches. I think the indies know that, in the best scenarios, Waterstones and the indies are mutually supportive."

Kelly Justice, who is the owner of the Fountain Bookstore in Richmond, Virginia, perfectly illustrated the horrors of online competition for an independent, when she found herself going viral after complaining on Twitter about the process of "showrooming," which sees people taking pictures of the carefully curated books in her store, and then going onto their phones to buy them from Amazon. "This is not ok, people. Find it here. Buy it here. Keep us here. That is all," she wrote on Twitter. Showrooming is still an issue today, Justice says, and "it's incredibly hurtful when people use your brain and your curation and your time, even your hospitality and kindness, and then boast about buying the book from somewhere else."

Online competition, agrees Kenny, is a major issue—although Kennys prides itself on being the first business in Ireland to go online in 1994. "Amazon is an ongoing challenge for us, both as a competitor and working with them as a third-party seller," says Kenny. "Like many others, we sell through their portals, but they take a large percentage of every sale. While they are the default option for so many people, the challenge for us and for the retail industry is to get people to buy direct off local companies outside of Amazon." To this end, Kennys offers free delivery worldwide and lower prices on thousands of books, as well as heavily promoting Irish books and publishing. "The strength and importance of current Irish literature is lost on Amazon," she says. "Our message is always to buy directly off us on Kennys.ie, where the service, price and quality is frequently better for the customer. There are a growing number of consumers who are looking for alternatives to Amazon for their online shopping—the 'shop local' message has certainly gained momentum and was hugely driven in Ireland for the Black Friday and Christmas season." Despite Amazon's ubiquitous reach, Halls feels that, like Kennys, independents are finding "their niche against online." "Bookstores were first into the Amazon firestorm," she says. "They've had 25 years to get used to it. The ones who are still around, there's only half as many, but they are stronger. They know how to appeal to their customers. They still get [annoyed], people still come into the showroom, people still come in and ask about a book and buy it on Amazon and it's just rude, frankly, but they know how to offer something different and that difference comes down to community, it comes down to personality, it comes down to being an asset for that high street that's way beyond the transactional relationship." Independents around the world also face the issue of finding the right staff: many of these stores become renowned for the knowledge and personality of their owners, from Brazenhead's late Michael Seidenberg to Shaun Bythell, who wrote a book about life as a bookseller in Scotland's Wigtown. In these cases, customers often come to visit partly to see the bookseller in charge. "The owner is part of the proposition, but they can't be there all the time," says Halls. "So how do you build a team when you can't afford to pay top dollar for salary? They recruit people who are passionate about books, and it does work a lot of the time, but it is challenging."

For Justice, in Virginia, the real challenge facing the book industry across the board "is our tendency to navel-gaze and just see the world from our tiny little place in it. The average person sees a book as a way to spend their free time: no higher or lower in status than streaming their favorite shows, playing video games, attending a sports event, going out to a new club, whatever. The book industry needs to understand that more deeply. "Until books are as likely to be discussed around the water cooler as the Super Bowl [...] we are not solving the problems of our industry. Everyone will benefit if there are more readers: bookstores, publishers, authors, and the new readers themselves."

Despite the challenges, Justice has no intention of stopping a job she has been doing for 30 years. "What means the most to me is connecting to people over the written word. It never gets old," she says. "Books and reading give us a unique way to connect with our humanity and with each other. When I finish a book I love, I can't wait to talk about it! Sharing that joy with others, as many people as possible, never gets old."

ALISON FLOOD is the books reporter for the Guardian. *She also reviews thrillers for the* Observer, *writes* The Bookseller's *monthly paperback preview, and freelances for a range of other publications on books. She loves shopping in independent bookstores.*

PRO QM

BERLIN · GERMANY

The revolution will be printed: this bookstore trusts in the combined forces of art, culture, and politics to bring about a fair future

TOP Tucked away in a side street behind Rosa-Luxemburg-Platz in Berlin, the location is befitting to this popular bookstore: Luxemburg was a philosopher and revolutionary socialist herself.

OPPOSITE Pro qm focuses on contemporary publications on urban policy, culture, and economics, along with architecture, art, and design.

Our most legendary event, in the early 2000s, was an evening with British dance icon Michael Clark and The Fall's Mark E. Smith, who performed in our space." No, you're not mistaken—we're talking about a bookstore here. But this is a Berlin bookstore, after all. Pro qm has been part of the German capital's art and cultural scene since 1999, providing food for thought, hosting panel discussions, and selling the right kind of reading material. "The store evolved from theoretical debates and discussions on urban politics and alternative spaces for cultural production, especially here in Berlin in the late nineties, into a physical location to engage in these issues with a wider public," says Katja Reichard, who today runs Pro qm alongside Jesko Fezer and Axel John Wieder as part of a team of seven. The impetus that led them to open the store was none other than a book.

If You Lived Here: The City in Art, Theory, and Social Activism was published to accompany a series of events and exhibitions organized by the artist Martha Rosler in New York in 1989. "The publication brings together artists, activists, planners, scientists, residents, and neighbors, documenting the crisis in New York's housing market in the late 1980s, while also presenting a broad range of analysis and strategies to counteract this," Reichard says. Focusing on the core theme of the city and its interfaces with politics, pop culture, business, architecture, design, sound, and art, Pro qm is building on precisely that legacy. That's a whole lot of revolution per square foot! 📖

PRO QM

TOP For over 20 years, Pro qm has been sparking interesting discussions among Berlin's urban policymakers and cultural scene.

LEFT The store and its inspiring selection of titles is managed by a seven-person team.

OPPOSITE Like all good things, this bookstore was kindled from a revolutionary spark.

IT'S A BOOK

LISBON · PORTUGAL

Book lovers from around the world fall into conversation between the bright shelves of this independent bookstore

Although It's a Book isn't organized into conventional sections like many bookstores, say António Alves and Joana Silva, "we do enjoy giving extra visibility to books from small, independent publishers, self-published works, and artists' editions. These publications often have unique and special qualities that prevent them from being produced by established publishers." Alves and Silva have run It's a Book since 2016, and although they focus on children's books, their books and workshop aren't solely aimed at small visitors. "We've always been of the opinion that children's books are not necessarily for children, and that they have great potential for crossing cultural and sociological divides," they say. "It was great to have this confirmed by our surprisingly diverse mix of customers and fans!" People with all sorts of viewpoints and ways of life meet in front of the bright shelves. What everyone has in common is an interest in children's books, and this can spark exciting discussions. "Not only are they different types and styles of people, they are also of varied ages, from children to seniors and including all the age groups in between. They are also from varied locations and cultures around the world, and they buy the books for a myriad of reasons. 📖

TOP Adult readers will also find plenty to delight them on the shelves of this children's bookstore in Portugal.

OPPOSITE Joana Silva and António Alves like to sell publications by artists, self-publishers, and independent publishing houses.

145

WILD RUMPUS

MINNEAPOLIS · MINNESOTA · USA

Tame chickens, rats, and chinchillas roam freely around this prize-winning children's bookstore

Collette Morgan and Tom Braun have created an utterly delightful children's bookstore in Wild Rumpus, inspired by two children's books. "Let the wild rumpus start!" cries young Max in the classic children's book *Where the Wild Things Are* by the American illustrator Maurice Sendak, who serves as a kind of godfather to Wild Rumpus. In terms of the atmosphere and design, Morgan and Braun drew upon the enchanting children's book *The Salamander Room* by the American writer Anne Mazer. The ceiling of the colorful store appears to have cracked open, offering a view of the sky, like something from a fairytale. A children's door is integrated into the violet entrance, allowing only small visitors through it.

Together with the lovingly curated books and packed program of events, the animals are the real stars at Wild Rumpus: between the shelves, Caldecott and Newbery, two fluffy chinchillas, scamper free. The black and white rats Mrs. Who, Mrs. Which, and Mrs. Whatsit live beneath a wooden plank in the horror section. Bold children can visit the tarantula, which is called Rubeus Hagrid, while others can cuddle up with the chicken or cats. Just like in the stories *The Salamander Room* and *Where the Wild Things Are,* in this bookstore, the boundaries between space, time, and nature are blurred. Wild Rumpus now inspires young readers and their parents in turn, encouraging them to see the world and its wonders with their eyes wide open. 📖

TOP The real stars of Wild Rumpus are the tame animals that run free among the books.

OPPOSITE This ambitious children's bookstore skillfully navigates the boundary between reality and fantasy.

147

CASA BOSQUES

MEXICO CITY · MEXICO

These two Mexican booksellers have
dedicated themselves to print, following their
own instincts, and chocolate desserts

My business partner Rafael and I both share a passion for print," says Jorge de la Garza. He has run Casa Bosques along-side Rafael Prieto since 2012. "We both moved to Mexico City around the same time and realized that although the art scene was very sophisti-cated, with many museums, galleries, [and] institutions, there wasn't really a specialized art and design bookstore in the city. So we decided to open one ourselves." Casa Bosques focuses on titles from independent publishing houses in Mexico, the USA, Europe, and Central and South America.

The clearly arranged shelves are filled with publications on art, architecture, photog-raphy, design, and theory, supplemented by a captivating selection of international maga-zines and sought-after fanzines. Beyond their bookstore business, Prieto and de la Garza are enthusiastic about the art of printing. The team have organized the Index Art Book Fair from its very first year in 2014; it has been an important platform for creative print products in Mexico City ever since then.

Casa Bosques also hosts regular events that venture into other genres of art. Previous highlights have included a book exhibition with a private concert by the psychedelic folk singer Devendra Banhart, who sat nonchalantly between the white shelving units and sang his songs. Kim Gordon of the American band Sonic Youth has also signed books here, says de la Garza. And to add a few extra delicacies to this visual and musical smorgasbord, Casa Bosques may be the only bookstore in the world to sell its own chocolate. 📖

LEFT To this day, the book launch with Devendra Banhart remains one of the owners' most fondly remembered events.

OPPOSITE The art and design bookstore concentrates on independent Mexican and international publications.

149

TOP Cactuses and other plants bring the outdoors inside, while also providing a reminder of the store's setting.

LEFT The Casa Bosques team has had a positive response to its practice of presenting its books with the covers on full display.

OPPOSITE The small bookstore is often used as a venue for art and music events.

WUGUAN BOOKS

KAOHSIUNG · TAIWAN

Under the cover of darkness, hidden desires—and some very special books— are brought to light

uguan Books isn't just a dark bookstore," says Chu Chih-kang, the designer behind the store: it's "a haven where everything in the mundane world is screened out and only the books that the soul seeks to read are left." That pretty much sums up the ethos behind the store. No glowing neon sign indicates that it's there at all, no display windows allow visitors to gaze in or out. Instead, roughly 400 books are displayed in the dark, each with its own little light. Faces of other customers remain shrouded in darkness. Thick carpets muffle any noise. The atmosphere is reminiscent of an intimate salon. "Everything that normally defines our day-to-day lives can be shelved here," explains the team. "After all, in the absence of visible social roles, we allow ourselves to be ourselves and follow our heart's desires." The range of titles lives up to these expectations, with inspiring works of predominantly adult literature, on themes like psychology and erotica. Hence why entry is restricted to people 18 and over. "With less person-to-person interference, visitors can choose whatever books they like to read without worrying about other people's judging eyes, as well as focusing on reading without disruption," adds the team. "Wuguan Books helps you open that door to your inner self. Once you go through it, a frank and authentic interaction with yourself awaits." 📖

BOTTOM Readers who come to browse in this bookstore can be sure that they'll go unnoticed: their faces remain in darkness.

OPPOSITE Each of the 400 titles at Wuguan Books is lit by its very own lamp.

153

WUGUAN BOOKS

TOP The feel of this bookstore is reminiscent of a private salon where people can put their public selves to one side.

LEFT The selection of titles at Wuguan Books is aimed at adult readers and ranges from psychology to erotica.

OPPOSITE The team hopes that its books and installations will encourage readers to take an honest look at themselves.

THE RIPPED BODICE

CULVER CITY · CALIFORNIA · USA

With help from a crowdfunding campaign, two sisters have opened a bookstore that sells only romance novels

TOP Bea (left, with dog Fitzwilliam Waffles) and Leah Koch (right) jointly run a thoroughly romantic bookstore.

OPPOSITE The sisters provide a wonderful platform for the magic of romance at The Ripped Bodice.

"Our bookstore is your all-knowing and incredibly loving aunt," say Bea and Leah Koch. "She gives you the best books you need to read to learn what good sex is and what you deserve in a relationship." The two sisters opened The Ripped Bodice—named for the title of Bea's master's thesis on romance novels—in 2016, off the back of a hugely successful Kickstarter campaign. They specialize exclusively in romance novels. "Romance is a very full world, so we're always trying to bring in new voices or stories we haven't seen before," explain the siblings. Indeed, there's huge demand for love stories. Even Sony Pictures is now working with the sisters, who have adapted various romance novels into TV series together. The lovingly furnished store in Culver City has already attracted a cult following, and Bea and Leah Koch say they are among the youngest independent book dealers in the world.

The two sisters say: "We love owning a romance-focused bookstore. It gives us a purpose and focus. Almost every day we hear the same thing: 'I've wanted this kind of bookstore my entire life,' and 'I've never read romance—where do I start?' It means everything to us to be there for both types of reader—those just starting their romance journey and life-long fans." 📖

157

THE RIPPED BODICE

TOP The managers are aware that romance is a wide-ranging genre and that there's a huge demand for love stories.

LEFT Stories to savor: visitors can enjoy browsing the selection of books over a literary cup of tea.

OPPOSITE Sony Pictures is interested in the Kochs' venture and is developing new TV series with the sisters.

159

HALPER'S BOOKS

TEL AVIV · ISRAEL

How 140 boxes of books and a plan B
resulted in a popular gathering
place in Tel Aviv for readers from
an array of cultures

In the early 1990s, having exhausted all other ideas for ways of making a living, Yosef Halper put all of his eggs in one basket and moved from New Jersey to Tel Aviv with 140 boxes of books. "It was the worst timing you could possibly imagine," says Halper today. "We landed right in the middle of the Gulf War. When the rocket attacks finally stopped, my wife and I swept the shards of glass out of our apartment and I went out to look for premises." He found what he was after in Allenby Street, which he describes as Tel Aviv's Broadway. Having started off with an English-language selection, he soon expanded his range to include books in Hebrew, plus other languages to cater to tourists from all over the world. The store has a conventional focus on history, philosophy, and literature. Halper listens to his own instincts when it comes to book-buying. Even if a book doesn't fly off the shelf, he knows that someone will come for it eventually. His shelves also hold valuable works from the private libraries of Israeli diplomats and ex-presidents. "Israel is a small country," he says. "It would be much harder to come by these kinds of items elsewhere." But what he loves most of all is the vibrant mix of customers who peruse the narrow aisles of Halper's Books, browsing and discussing together, and often discovering that there is much more that unites them than divides them. 📖

LEFT Halper's Books has been based in traditional Allenby Street in Tel Aviv since the early 1990s.

OPPOSITE Yosef Halper and his daughter Sara in their element: steeped in history and surrounded by stories.

HALPER'S BOOKS

TOP To this day, Halper's Books remains one of the beloved haunts of Tel Aviv's intercultural scene.

LEFT Ravens have symbolized wisdom and been seen as conveyors of news for millennia.

OPPOSITE The much-photographed little outpost of Halper's Books, which also serves as a signpost.

UNDER THE COVER

LISBON · PORTUGAL

This Portuguese book and magazine store relies on strong covers and tells the stories of the people behind the publications

LEFT The little bookstore brings customers together with the publishers of the magazines on display.

OPPOSITE Under the Cover has been in business since 2015 between the Museu Calouste Gulbenkian and the adjacent park.

Editors are pushing the boundaries of what a magazine can be, creating exciting content paired with astonishing design and visuals," explains Luís Cunha. He and Arturas Slidziauskas have run the minimalist-style book and magazine store Under the Cover in Lisbon since 2015. The store, which features a white and blue façade, is located between the Museu Calouste Gulbenkian and its park. Here, architecture, nature, and art are fused together beneath the Portuguese sun.

Those with an interest in culture attend book launches, creative events, and evenings of conversation with media specialists at the store. "One of our aims when opening the bookshop was to inspire locals to work as contributors to the magazines we stock, or to start their own publication," Cunha says. "Today, we're proud to say we've seen some examples of this. Things have come full circle, and it feels really good." He sees magazines as a key component of contemporary culture and, by the same token, important time capsules. "As shop owners," he said, "we get to know the editors, their stories, and all the effort they put into the magazines. We tell their stories to our customers, bringing them closer to the objects, but also to their makers."

CINNOBER

COPENHAGEN · DENMARK

This artbook gallery with a holistic approach spoils Copenhagen with its carefully chosen titles on craft and design

LEFT Ulla Welinder's little basement store lies right beside the Rundetårn, the astronomical tower in Copenhagen.

BOTTOM Together with a choice selection of art and design books, Cinnober also sells exquisite stationery and covetable paraphernalia.

OPPOSITE The key criteria for stocking every item in the range is its quality and value.

As a trained graphic and textile designer, Ulla Welinder, the owner of Cinnober, has a trained eye and a real feel for beautiful handmade items. Opulent tomes like *Textiles of Japan,* on the collection of Thomas Murray, and *Breathing Patterns,* a catalogue of work by the Filipino artist Marina Cruz, adorn the white shelves of her basement store near Copenhagen's Rundetårn. "Beside their content, I find art and design books to be wonderful objects," explains Welinder. "Paper quality, binding, printing, cover design, and content add up to a complete experience," she says. "To make a space for this and to share all of it with customers is a special privilege." A selection of stationery complements the range of books. Yet Welinder's loyal clientele also appreciate Cinnober for its calming atmosphere. "I have experienced customers entering, and, after browsing books and paper goods for a while, they breathe in, their shoulders relax, and they say, 'Oh, how I needed a dose of Cinnober!'" 📖

10 CORSO COMO
MILAN · ITALY

When a grande dame of the Italian
fashion scene curates her own
bookstore, extravagance is *de rigeur*

ocated in a traditional Milan *palazzo*, this bookstore shines resplendent as part of a luxurious overall concept—the brainchild of an equally dazzling art collector, gallerist, and fashion editor. Carla Sozzani lives and breathes style, fashion, and design, having worked as editor-in-chief of various fashion magazines. Indeed, she counts many influential photographers among her circle of friends. She curates her world-famous concept store, 10 Corso Como, with a consummate sense of style. Books are an indispensable part of life for the Italian. That's why the bookstore and gallery form the heart of the store:

Sozzani has "structured a living magazine, where editorial choices in food and fashion, music and art, and lifestyle and design are constantly made by the visitor and customer." The selection of books is a clear reflection of Sozzani's fashion background. Large-format tomes about fashion designers like Pierre Cardin, Azzedine Alaïa, and Manolo Blahnik are ranged alongside publications on art, design, architecture, and photography. Pops of color and eye-catching design elements are everywhere to be seen. Insider tip: you can retreat to the in-store café or the courtyard garden with a newly acquired treasure. 📖

OPPOSITE The glamorous Milan property that houses 10 Corso Como also includes a wonderful courtyard garden.

BOTTOM Art expert Carla Sozzani designed the bookstore as part of her legendary overall concept.

169

POWELL'S BOOKS

PORTLAND · OREGON · USA

A destination for book fanatics:
this family-run bookstore occupies an entire
block with its vast selection of books

TOP With over two million books, Powell's Books has the biggest selection of any bookstore in the United States.

OPPOSITE The family-run enterprise now has 550 employees and five bookstores in and around Portland.

Visiting our flagship bookstore has been compared to looking over the edge of the Grand Canyon," says Emily Powell. "It's a moving experience entering a world of books that takes up a full city block." Powell is now in charge of the famous bookstore, which has the largest collection of books in the United States, at over 2 million titles. Powell's Books was founded in 1971 by her grandfather Walter Powell and later continued by her father, Michael Powell.

"My grandfather taught me that our job is to connect the writer's voice with the reader's ear and not let our egos get in between," says the bookseller. "My father taught me not only the love of the book itself but also how to love the business of bookselling." Nearly 550 employees now work at the five Powell's bookstores in and around Portland. "We have an especially intimate relationship with Portland," enthuses Powell. "What other city in America can name a bookstore as its top attraction?" The city certainly has it right. Powell's Books hosts over 500 author events a year, while the very youngest readers are invited to storytime sessions. Writing workshops, game demonstrations, and book clubs complete the packed program of cultural events.

"As a child, I recall riding with my grandfather in the truck that picked up and delivered books," remembers Powell. "It was my dream, when I grew up, to drive the 'bookie truck,' and in many ways, that's exactly what I'm doing today." 📖

LEFT Emily Powell is a third-generation member of the family behind the bookstores, which enrich Portland's cultural scene with countless events.

BOTTOM Powell's Books hosts over 500 events every year, from readings and workshops to play sessions.

OPPOSITE Powell's grandfather came up with the ambitious idea for the successful bookstore and founded it in 1971.

HOW DO THEY DO IT?

The more niche, the better: why specialized bookstores not only exist, but are thriving

Boatbuilding instructions, treatises on oceanography, and biographies of seafarers pack the shelves of the Libreria del Mare in Milan. The little bookstore specializes in literature relating to the seas, and it has not only stayed afloat since 1973 but also progressively expanded its range. The Libreria del Mare is one of those fascinating niche bookstores whose special concepts make them both remarkable and successful. Any attempt at specialization is a balancing act, after all. Does the selection stand out enough, or does it go too far the other way—too off-the-wall? Is its clientele likely to remain interested in a particular topic over a long period of time? Does the bookstore's niche provide the potential to offer a constant flow of new literature and inspiration? Is it not yet completely saturated?

"Our strength is the professional competence of our booksellers' team" says Alessandro Gigliola, who runs the Libreria del Mare alongside two other fans of all things nautical, "able to guide the reader to the right choice depending on his tastes and necessities, through the deep knowledge of our publications and products." Sea-loving writers regularly read in the Milan bookstore. In addition, the Libreria del Mare collaborates with various private and public institutions,

thus bringing together like-minded people, regardless of age, profession, or nationality.

Anyone who gears their bookstore specifically towards a certain theme will have a narrower base than generalists with broad appeal. At the same time, their energy will not be spread across a range, but rather concentrated on a specific point. In other words, the smaller the niche, the more profound the knowledge of the person behind it. And it is precisely this depth of expertise that ensures its success. From a purely logical point of view, one thing is clear: those who dedicate themselves to a particular topic or special field are able to stock books and offer recommendations in a more focused way. There's a reason that most customers head for a niche bookstore if they're seeking tailor-made advice and inspiration. This is better still when passed from person to person, rather than via a computer-generated algorithm. The chance of discovering more interesting titles in a niche bookstore is greatly increased due to the very nature of such places. And quite apart from that, such stores promise readers the unique delight of being able to immerse themselves completely in the realm that captivates them.

Some 300 miles from the Libreria del Mare, Librairie Imbernon in Marseille

deals exclusively in books on architecture, with corresponding art and design publications. This specialist bookstore is, rather fittingly, housed in a major UNESCO-protected building by star architect Le Corbusier. Owner Katia Imbernon publishes architecture books herself, while her husband is an architect, historian, and professor at the École Nationale Supérieur d'Architecture de Marseille. "This place, which is regularly visited by experts and architecture fans from every continent, was simply crying out for our bookstore," says Imbernon. She selects the range of titles on the strict basis that they must be informative publications about 20th-century architecture. Handpicked titles, rare editions, classics, and new releases cover a wide spectrum of topics, from functionalism to Bauhaus and postmodernism. Expert knowledge and heartfelt passion have formed the foundation of this bookstore's long existence.

On the other side of the Channel, the popular bookstore Treadwell's specializes in the occult. The store is stuffed to the brim with new, rare, and antiquarian books about magic, alchemy, applied sorcery, astrology, instructions for performing rituals, and magic accessories. Thanks to special events like readings, tarot card consultations, and shamanic meetings, a small community has formed around the London bookstore, and it is constantly growing. "Someone recently gave us the greatest compliment by saying we have become the most famous esoteric bookstore in the world," owner Christina Oakley Harrington says delightedly. She has transformed her own passion into her dream career. Along with the right book for them, customers also benefit from the invaluable knowledge of a woman who has been dealing with magic for decades. The New York bookstore Bluestockings sells books on LGBTQ + themes, Black Power, climate protection, and global equity. Marginalized groups and the target audience are one and the same thing here.

The bookstore sees itself as an active part of a radical feminist movement and serves as a protected space for many customers, where they are able to give their personalities free rein. Matilda Sabal is one of the many activist volunteers who run the feminist bookstore and events space. Years ago, she went to Bluestockings with the express purpose of delving deeper into the subject of equality for people with disabilities. The fact that she works here today is testament to the inspiring selection of titles and the supportive community that has sprung up around the niche bookstore. She says: "For me, and I think for many other people, Bluestockings is one of the first times they feel truly seen,

and see their struggles and identity reflected in the space around them."

We know that a bookstore can be centered around a single theme, but where do you go from there? The Japanese bookstore Morioka Shoten has adopted a hyper-minimalist concept that is just as fantastical as it sounds—the store sells a single book. Or, to be precise, multiple copies of a single title, which changes weekly. Owner Yoshiyuki Morioka relies on concentration and slow reading as a means of familiarizing readers with the work of the author in question. By concentrating fully on a single title, he hopes to nourish the essential joy of reading among customers. →

LEFT Morioka Shoten bookstore in Tokyo sells just one book.

THERE'S A REASON THAT MOST CUSTOMERS HEAD FOR A NICHE BOOKSTORE IF THEY'RE SEEKING TAILOR-MADE ADVICE AND INSPIRATION.

BOOKSTORES RELY ON PEOPLE WHO MEET, CHAT, AND THINK BETWEEN THE SHELVES.

→ And the much-feared online giant? As it differs from niche bookstores in so many fundamental respects—service, expertise, and experience—it doesn't actually represent competition. Businesses that can win customers over by offering a complete package will survive. That said, niche bookstores do have to move with the times. Most of them have online shops where they present and sell their books. Photos are uploaded and invitations to special events issued via social media. Tradition and development are not mutually exclusive. What's more, niche bookstores rely to a greater extent than their mainstream counterparts on the community of people who meet, chat, and think between the shelves. When there are magical soirées with like-minded people, talks on oceanography against a backdrop of old ships' wheels and compasses, or expert discussions with a professor of architecture in a UNESCO World Heritage-listed building, selling books is almost an afterthought. None of this can happen on the internet, of course. Exchanging views, getting involved, revolutionary discussions in a bookstore aimed at marginalized groups, or simply indulging in the experience of not having to make a choice at all, but having just one book before you: these are all experiences that can only take place in niche bookstores.

Travel writer MARIANNE JULIA STRAUSS has scoured the globe for the past decade in search of the top bookstores. In Do You Read Me? *she has collected a selection of the ones you need to include in your next itinerary.*

177

KRUMULUS

BERLIN · GERMANY

Don't grow up, it's a trap:
this Berlin children's bookstore is the
best remedy against growing old

LEFT These letters aren't just for reading, but can even be picked up: the store has its own printing workshop.

BOTTOM At the popular workshops, children can do activities like printing their own backpacks with bright lettering.

OPPOSITE Celebrating Pippi Longstocking-style! The children's bookstore is renowned for its colorful parties.

D ear little Krumalura, I don't want to grow up, never ever." With those words, Pippi Longstocking and her friends Tommy and Annika swallow the mysterious Krummelus pills so that they never have to become boring old adults. Just as well that some adults aren't all that boring at all, but instead open wonderful children's bookstores with almost the same name as Pippi's anti-growing-up pills. Anna Morlinghaus has run Krumulus as a bookstore, secondhand children's bookseller, gallery, printing workshop, and reading room since 2014. "Krumulus is a place for children," explains the owner and mother of four boys. "Everything should be friendly, playful, easily accessible, and directly tangible. At Krumulus you can look at everything, and touch almost everything, too." This principle also feeds into the selection of the books, which are suitable for children to read for themselves or have read to them, and cover everything a child could desire, from excitement to humor. With that in mind, Morlinghaus has put together a vibrant program for children, with over 250 events per year. Regular exhibitions by children's book illustrators, creative courses, readings, printing workshops, concerts, and theater performances delight, encourage, and challenge young →

179

ANTIQUARIAT
DRUCKWERKSTATT

→ readers. Morlinghaus is a trained graphic designer and has long run a gallery in Berlin. "When I had my first child, I discovered a great love of stories and illustration," recalls the bookseller. Today there's hardly enough room for all of the titles that are important to her in the store. "Children make a fantastic clientele. They're curious, enthusiastic, funny, unpredictable, thoroughly honest, sometimes exhausting, but always fresh. Once you've grown up for good, it's nice to surround yourself with lots of little Krumulants."

TOP Krumulus owner Anna Morlinghaus has created a vibrant wonderland for little readers.

OPPOSITE Krumulus is at once a bookstore, seller of antiquarian children's books, gallery, printing workshop, and reading room.

181

BILDERBOX

VIENNA · AUSTRIA

This comic store in Vienna is dedicated
to graphic novels and illustrated art books—
and bright, graffiti-inspired accessories

Displayed on the white shelves at Bilderbox, the comics and illustrated books look like little works of art in their own right. They are interspersed with brightly colored spray cans, jet-black markers, sketchbooks, brushes, and an array of inks and paints for customers who fancy exercising their own artistic streak. Owner Malte Steinhausen exemplifies that very concept within the store, having created everything about Bilderbox himself, right down to the interior fittings. "I was 30 when I opened the store, and I didn't have the slightest experience," he said. "But I was lucky enough to do it at a time when street art and graphic novels were becoming popular." Steinhausen's favorite songs play in the background as customers rummage through the superbly curated selection of products: "That's another reason why I love running Bilderbox so much." The books include plenty of Steinhausen's most cherished titles, such as Winschluss's merciless new take on the tale of *Pinocchio*. "You have to be a bit off-the-wall to open a bookstore," says Steinhausen knowingly. "After all, Christmas only comes once a year!" 📖

TOP Feeling inspired? The bookstore also sells artists' accessories for graffiti art and more.

BOTTOM A façade like an open book: Bilderbox sells the most visually appealing and exciting graphic novels and comics.

LEFT It goes without saying that owner Malte Steinhausen is a consummate graphic novel fan himself.

BOTTOM A shelf like a little treasure trove: Pascal Rabaté's tranquil, lovingly drawn graphic novels are a perennial highlight.

OPPOSITE Bilderbox has really committed to the DIY principle: from the counter to the shelving, everything here has been custom-made.

MORIOKA SHOTEN

TOKYO · JAPAN

This Japanese bookstore sells just one book. Yes, really: a single title.

It is often said that the Japanese have perfected the art of minimalism. Yoshiyuki Morioka has now applied this concept to an area that would, at first glance, appear wholly unsuited to it. His bookstore, Morioka Shoten, sells just one book. Or, to be more precise, a number of copies of a single title, which changes on a weekly basis. Morioka worked as a bookseller for many years before presenting his idea at a business event hosted by the design agency Takram in 2014—in minimalistic style, of course, on a single sheet of paper. The agency was thrilled. The designers worked together with the bookseller to develop the idea into a real store. "Morioka Shoten, a single room with a single book" reads the slogan, which sums up the enterprise to perfection. The bookstore is successful not despite but precisely because of the utter straightforwardness of its wares—and has since become a minor attraction in its own right. 📖

TOP The shop's wares could hardly be more strikingly arranged: after all, Morioka Shoten sells only a single title at a time.

OPPOSITE Yoshiyuki Morioka's extraordinary bookstore exemplifies the principle of minimalism to superb effect.

187

PRINTED MATTER

NEW YORK CITY · USA

Get printing: a group of artists discovered
the book as an art form in the 1970s and were
inspired to set up a bookstore

LEFT The bookstore, which is run by artists, lies on 11th Avenue, just a block from the Hudson River.

BOTTOM Printed Matter's stated mission is to increase appreciation for artistic publications.

OPPOSITE The book has been used as an art form since the 1960s. Printed Matter showcases the most exciting works to be published.

Victor Hugo believed that the invention of the printing press was the most significant event in the history of the world. The eight owners of Printed Matter take a similar view, having dedicated an entire bookstore to this momentous invention.

The store has existed since 1976 as a nonprofit organization geared towards the promotion and appreciation of artists' books. "Printed Matter was developed in response to the growing interest in publications made by artists," explains the team, which now welcomes interested visitors at its premises on 11th Avenue, following several moves. "Starting in the early sixties, artists began to explore the possibilities of the book form as an artistic medium. Large-edition and economically produced publications allowed experimentation with artworks that were affordable and could circulate outside of the mainstream gallery system." To this day, Printed Matter celebrates unusual, creative, and surprising books as complex and meaningful artworks, helping to provide a wonderful platform for this once-underrated form of art. 📖

BLUESTOCKINGS

NEW YORK CITY · USA

This radical feminist bookstore
fights for a rainbow world with love,
passion, and literature

Bluestockings is a labor of love. It is run by volunteers who believe that it is important for radical spaces like this to continue to exist," says Matilda Sabal, one of the many volunteer activists who run the feminist bookstore and event space in New York.

Since 1999, the bookstore has followed the tradition of the Bluestockings—the intellectual women who struggled for emancipation and women's rights from the mid-19th century. The volunteers describe their collective bookstore as a "radical feminist bookstore and activist space." For many of them, it has become a home away from home and a judgement-free, protective place.

The range of books and packed program of events range from LGBTQ+ themes to Black Power, from climate protection to global justice. An eclectic, engaged community gathers in the fair trade café for author readings, political discussions, and open-gender workshops. "We strive to make Bluestockings an environment where everyone feels safe. We carry books that would be hidden away in the back of other bookstores, if other stores carried them at all," says Sabal.

"For me, and I think for many other people, this bookstore was one of the first places where I felt truly seen." 📖

TOP The bookstore is named after the Bluestockings, a historical name for people campaigning for an emancipated society.

BOTTOM Bluestockings sells a wide array of publications that run the gamut from feminist topics to Black Power and environmental protection.

OPPOSITE The New York bookstore has been going strong since 1999 with the help of lots of activist volunteers.

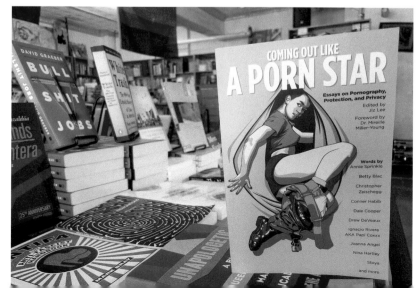

PROUST
WÖRTER+TÖNE

ESSEN · GERMANY

The bricks-and-mortar and literature-on-wheels incarnations of this plastic-free bookstore are happy to help customers in their search for an engrossing book

Marcel Proust's *Pleasures and Days* would certainly have featured on the shelves of this bookstore. Proust Wörter + Töne is a cultural institution in the Ruhr region. "Every six months, we put together a new selection of books with subjects that we find stirring," say Peter Kolling and Beate Scherzer, who have run the independent bookstore in Essen since 2005. "We might choose from independent publishing houses that give us a fresh insight into ourselves from the outside in, or which urge us to be open to literary diversity or compelling cultural diagnoses." Such wonderful encouragement is only sweetened by the homemade cakes served by the friendly Café Livres and an excellent music section. The "Töne" ("sound") bit of the equation comes in the form of classical music and jazz. The bookstore team sates visitors' thirst for culture with events at which even literary heavyweights like T. C. Boyle and Herta Müller have been known to appear and join in the discussion.

The bookstore is also deliberately plastic-free: the team issues paper and fabric bags only, and actively encourages publishers to refrain from shrink-wrapping their books. And that's not all: it also offers a free delivery service by bike or Proust-mobile. "Some people are unable to visit the store in person for various reasons, but we might still want to make them our customers or keep supplying them with reading matter if they're no longer as mobile as they'd like to be," says the staff. Twice a week, the team hits the road and delights people with lovely books, great wine, and, not infrequently, a living-room chat. "Everyone's a winner!" beam Kolling and Scherzer. The fact that they win the German Bookstore Awards year after year is a testament to their success. After all, as long-established publisher Klaus Wagenbach says: "Only in a bookstore like Proust are you likely to chance upon books that you weren't looking for—but definitely need."

TOP Peter Kolling and his team regularly travel out to less-mobile customers in their Proust-mobile.

OPPOSITE Literature, music, events, and a sustainable approach await behind the floor-to-ceiling glass façade of Proust Wörter + Töne.

193

WHAT'S THE MAGIC WORD?

TREADWELL'S · LONDON · UNITED KINGDOM

This magical bookstore encourages new perspectives and introduces curious visitors to the arcane world of wisdom and magic

RIGHT Those looking for advice, entertainment, or magical company flock to the weekly tarot evenings.

OPPOSITE With a selection of books focused on magic, this store fulfills a longing as old as mankind itself.

The occult has long been a significant, if often secret, part of the cultures of our world. Christina Oakley-Harrington has dedicated her extraordinary bookstore to precisely those mysteries. Visitors interested in all things mystic will discover books about Celtic and African magic, astrology, alchemy, and applied witchcraft, not to mention tarot sets and supplies for magic rituals.

"Our specialty is the occult, which has its own special glamor: the country's leading druid once held a book launch with us, and attended in long robes, while young feminists come in to find books on witchcraft to dismantle the patriarchy," smiles the owner. The downstairs meditation room is rented out for shamanic ceremonies, pagan weddings, and rituals to summon the angels. The British folk-rock band Mumford and Sons also launched their career with their "Bookshop Sessions" at Treadwell's. "It was a wonderful experience," recalls the owner. "As far as we're concerned, magic encompasses the arts in a broader sense."

Oakley-Harrington opened Treadwell's in 2003, following a long career in academia. Naturally, her premises on the tree-lined Store Street in Bloomsbury is protected by a benevolent guardian spirit. "Our patron saint is Lady Wisdom," she explains. A little shrine within the store is dedicated to wisdom personified as a woman, as depicted by the alchemist Michael Maier in his 1618 work *Atalanta Fugiens*. "In the image, she issues forth from her hands prosperity and abundance, wisdom and occult secrets; she is our guiding spirit."

The inspiration for the bookstore came from the great Parisian salons of the 18th century, where friendships were forged and the seeds of revolutions sown. In keeping with this tradition, →

195

OUR PATRON SAINT IS LADY WISDOM. A LITTLE SHRINE WITHIN THE STORE IS DEDICATED TO WISDOM PERSONIFIED AS A WOMAN.

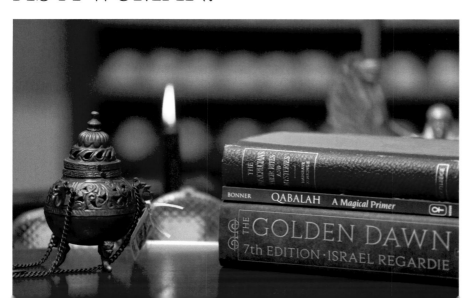

TOP AND LEFT Treadwell's sells ritual accessories and paraphernalia alongside books on everything from alchemy to magic.

OPPOSITE TOP Interested newbies and seasoned shamans and magicians meet in the aisles.

OPPOSITE BOTTOM Not only does Treadwell's sell magic books, but it also preserves an often-suppressed part of our cultures.

→ the bookstore hosts at least one soirée, reading, or other event every week. These events are Treadwell's lifeblood. "Bookshops ... are places of resistance, home to the new writers, and also keepers of the history of writing," says Oakley-Harrington, pointing to the framed quote by Heinrich Heine hanging on the wall: "Whenever they start burning books, they will end up burning people." She adds, "We are honored custodians and, at the same time, matchmakers. We will find the perfect book for every seeking reader as best we can, for to be a reader is to be a lover in search of the beloved." 📖

TREADWELL'S

TOP AND LEFT Treadwell's has gained worldwide renown for its exquisite selection of wares, ranging from standard reference books to complete rarities.

OPPOSITE TOP The enchanting bookstore has been running and constantly expanding its range since 2003.

OPPOSITE BOTTOM Treadwell's sees itself as both the guardian and mediator of the knowledge stored within.

ANALOG

BERLIN · GERMANY

Three publishers, a store, and a furniture maker have taken over a former gallery in Berlin with their enthusiasm for an analog world

What a character! The beating heart of the collectively run flagship store Analog, on bustling Potsdamer Straße, is the heavy Korrex printing press—everything here revolves around printed words and images. "We want to encourage reading and using analog products—books, magazines, notebooks," says Erik Spiekermann.

When the gallery beside his printing workshop became vacant, the graphic designer teamed up with the publishing houses Gestalten, Niggli, and Kehrer, the Berlin magazine store do you read me?! and furniture maker Nils Holger Moormann to open the Analog store. Its shelves are packed with letterpress blocks, cups, keyrings, notebooks, and postcards relating to printing and typography. There's also a fitting selection of design and reference books. "They [the books] contain all human knowledge and have two functions," says Spiekermann. "One, content. Two, object. A good book has to have both. It needs to work as a beautiful object and have something to say."

ANALOG

TOP Erik Spiekermann (left) with the limited-edition "Weltformat" print created using the Johannisberg high-speed printing press.

LEFT Of course, the range of books includes titles devoted to printing techniques, typography, layout, and design.

OPPOSITE Analog belongs to p98a, the printing workshop next door, which hosts regular tours and workshops.

203

LA LIBRERIA DEL MARE

MILAN · ITALY

20,000 books about the sea—adventurers and fans of the sea will find a fantastic haul of publications about the oceans here

Olives, cheeses, and confectionery once crammed the historic cherrywood shelves of this charming store. Today it sells treats for the mind instead: the Libreria del Mare specializes in books about the sea and has captured the hearts of countless seafarers. "Our bookshop is a little group of sea enthusiasts and passionate booksellers," says Alessandro Gigliola, who runs the Milan bookstore alongside Piera Casari and Simona Torriani. "[We want] to share with others this love for [the] ocean and nature. ... Our bookshop is not just a place where you buy books; it's a harbor from the stressful lifestyle of urban routine. It's a quiet oasis of peace, where every sea enthusiast can take a break and smell, for a while, the salty scent of the ocean." And Gigliola means this almost literally, as the Libreria del Mare has a charmingly maritime-based design. Compasses, marine-themed posters, and other essential ocean paraphernalia enhance the rich selection of books.

The team especially loves the children's books section. Young readers and sailors alike come here for informative books that the teams rate particularly highly. There is also a section of rare, valuable books about the sea. For real seafarers, though, the range of logbooks and nautical charts, which are still used in navigation today, are bound to prove the main draw. The Libreria del Mare is also involved in the Ocean Film Festival Italia and Urban Blue City Milan. Ship ahoy! 📖

TOP Every square inch is redolent of the salty sea air: from the book titles to the décor, everything here is dedicated to the high seas.

OPPOSITE This libreria is a veritable safe port for fans of the sea. Remarkably, it is over 90 miles from the nearest coast.

LA LIBRERIA DEL MARE

TOP All at sea in Milan! Among other ventures, the team is involved in the Ocean Film Festival Italia.

RIGHT Ocean prints, compasses, and maritime accessories complement the selection of books.

OPPOSITE Seasoned sailors will also find ships' logs and nautical charts at the Libreria del Mare.

THE BEATING HEART AND POETIC SOUL OF AMERICA

CITY LIGHTS BOOKSELLERS & PUBLISHERS
SAN FRANCISCO · CALIFORNIA · USA

As the publisher of the very first works of the Beat Poets, critics of the Vietnam War, and environmental activists, this bookstore has been synonymous with literary resistance for decades

RIGHT To this day, the selection of titles at City Lights includes radical, left-leaning, and revolutionary writings.

OPPOSITE The bookstore, which was founded in 1953, owes its name to the famous Charlie Chaplin movie *City Lights.*

The truth is that they only set out to sell paperbacks. When they sealed the founding of City Lights in 1953, with a handshake and five hundred dollars each, Lawrence Ferlinghetti and Peter D. Martin could never have imagined that this idea would give rise to one of the most influential bookstores in the world. Word soon got out about this engaging store in the midst of San Francisco's thriving art scene. "Once we opened up the doors, we could hardly get them closed at night—the place was always packed!" says present-day manager and publisher Elaine Katzenberger, quoting the founder Ferlinghetti, who established his own publishing house hot on the heels of City Lights.

Katzenberger started working at City Lights as a temp several decades ago. Today, her responsibilities include the publishing house, which was the first to publish legendary works like *Howl and Other Poems* by the American Beat poet Allen Ginsberg. "So during the 1950s, we published some of the very first books by poets who became the Beat Generation," she says. "During the 1960s and early 1970s, it was resistance to the Vietnam War, the environmental movement, experimenting with spiritual traditions—what's thought of as hippie culture and ideals. In the Reagan years, the focus was on the wars in Central America and anti-nuke movements." City Lights is at once "a historic institution and very much a living, breathing participant in contemporary society: that's the dance we do here."

Ferlinghetti, who became the sole proprietor of City Lights in 1955, made a succession of bold, avant-garde publishing decisions that garnered him a reputation as a visionary free spirit, but it also resulted in his arrest on several occasions. With his bookstore/publishing model, Katzenberger says, Ferlinghetti was able not →

209

LEFT Besides the books, the mementos that adorn the walls also have stories to tell.

OPPOSITE TOP Bookselling legend, publisher, and writer Lawrence Ferlinghetti has long been a social critic and member of the avant garde.

OPPOSITE BOTTOM The shelves are stocked with books including Allen Ginsberg's most famous work, *Howl and Other Poems,* which was first published by City Lights.

WE ARE AT ONCE A HISTORIC INSTITUTION AND VERY MUCH A LIVING, BREATHING PARTICIPANT IN CONTEMPORARY SOCIETY.

→ only to disseminate his ideas in San Francisco but also to make the books he published known on a national, and even international, stage. The press is still publishing contemporary, revolutionary, and critical works by local and international authors through its City Lights Pocket Poets series. The bookstore sees itself as part of a long tradition of resistance and freedom of speech in the United States, as is clear from the selection of books on its shelves. "The craft of bookselling lies not so much in reacting to the marketplace as in developing it, by representing, on our shelves, a point of view that sets us apart," explains Katzenberger. "As independent booksellers, we place the final plank in the bridge that connects the writer to the reader." To that end, City Lights concentrates on world literature, poetry, the arts, and progressive politics. The bookstore also supports lesser-known and emerging writers as well as independent presses. "Human beings are looking for collaboration—or commiseration—and stories," concludes Katzenberger. "Even though the experience of writing a book or reading a book can be a very personal and solitary project, a book is a record of our communal experience. So, a bookstore is like a storehouse for our souls."

The bookstore's renown is such that the little passageway to the left
of it bears the name of a good friend: Jack Kerouac Alley.

CĂRTUREȘTI CARUSEL

BUCHAREST · ROMANIA

This fairytale bookstore in the heart of the Romanian capital has brought an enchanted palace back to life

Cărturești Carusel doesn't just tell the stories of the books spread across the four dazzling white floors of its history-steeped home. This extraordinary bookstore also relates the storied past of this building, which has recently been given a new lease on life. In the early twentieth century, it belonged to the influential Chrissoveloni banking family. "The building was nationalized during the communist regime," say Serban Radu and Nicoleta Iordan, who now run Cărturești Carusel. After the revolution, it stood empty for a long time, until—in a state of severe dilapidation—it was restored to the heirs of the Chrissoveloni family. Huge investment and over 20,000 hours of labor were required to save the building. The restoration project was entrusted to the firm of architects Square One, which gave the building its modern look while respecting its history. Having been closed for a quarter of a century, the doors were finally reopened in 2015. The delightful building has been open to the public as a bookstore ever since.

Spread across more than 10,000 square feet, Cărturești Carusel is a dream come true for book lovers and fans of good design. On the top floor is a bistro, while the basement is home to a multimedia space. A gallery on the first floor hosts exhibitions of contemporary Romanian art. Together with Cărturești Carusel, Radu and Iordan also run a number of other bookstores in Romania. Their unique combination of carefully selected titles, design, and events, which range from book launches to wine tastings, have garnered them a loyal and largely young clientele. "We see ourselves as curators offering a cultural gathering place," they say. Their main achievement: "making reading cool again."

Buying books should be an "experience," they continue. "We have paid a lot of attention to architecture, interior design, lighting, and visual identity, so that each Cărturești has a unique design concept behind it, created by renowned Romanian architects and designers, or by young emerging artists." Radu and Iordan's establishments are increasingly featured in international →

CĂRTUREȘTI CARUSEL

→ publications showcasing Europe's most beautiful bookstores. Cărturești Carusel is often dubbed "the most Instagrammable bookstore in the world." From the early days, they say, "the bookstore succeeded in attracting the young trendsetters of Bucharest's fast-growing urban culture, giving them a forum where they can feel free to learn, to get in touch with each other, to read, to experiment, to create projects and events together." 📖

LEFT The architecture appears to frame the views within this historic building. The restoration of its four floors is an absolute masterpiece.

BOTTOM Among other things, the illuminated bookstore basement is home to a multimedia area.

OPPOSITE The majestic building stood empty for a quarter of a century before the state returned it to its rightful heirs.

BAHRISONS

NEW DELHI · INDIA

When the vicissitudes of life brought a
resourceful bookseller to New Delhi, a tale of
flight became an incredible success story

Balraj Bahri has a created a rich legacy. In 1953, in the wake of the partition of India, he opened Bahrisons in a New Delhi district populated by displaced people. Today, his store in the Khan Market is one of the top literary hotspots in the Indian capital. It now has three offshoots: the Bahrisons Kids Store and two other bookstores with in-house cafés. An independent publishing house and literary agency have also joined Bahri's stable of enterprises. On their guiding principle, Anuj Bahri quotes Mr. Bahri Sr.: "Books are like food: they satisfy your hunger for knowledge."

He runs the business alongside his mother, Bhag Malhotra, his wife, Rajni Malhotra, and their daughter, the writer Aanchal Malhotra. The ceiling-high shelves at Bahrisons are stocked with copies of Aanchal's widely acclaimed book *Remnants of a Separation*, which looks at her grandfather's flight, along with modern classics like *City of Djinns* by New Delhi-based Scottish historian William Dalrymple. According to the family, Bahri used to say, "The bookshop is like a good restaurant. The décor, the seating, the ambiance, and the service are all important when we go out to dine, but most important of all is the chef's ability to maintain the quality of the food that you are served. This is what brings you back again and again. And so it is with books—display, presentation, and service are essential, but most important is a personal knowledge of each customer and the ability to provide the books that meet his needs." 📖

BAHRISONS

TOP The family business now extends to four bookstores, a publishing house, and a literary agency.

LEFT The wide range of titles at Bahrisons includes Indian literature and international publications.

OPPOSITE Founder Balraj Bahri would say that "a bookstore is like a good restaurant." He considered recommending the right books to be an art in its own right.

LIBRAIRIE MOLLAT

BORDEAUX · FRANCE

How France's oldest independent
bookstore is bridging the gap between
tradition and modernity

RIGHT The Librairie Mollat has become famous on Instagram for its "bookfaces."

OPPOSITE The bookstore with its blue window frames is just 400 meters from the Cathédrale St. André.

For a bookstore today to be run by the fifth generation of the same family makes it something of a sensation. Founded in 1896, the Librairie Mollat is now the oldest independent bookstore in France. Denis Mollat oversees the company as general director, as well as holding various illustrious positions in business and politics. It's no wonder that, since 2003, he has been the first bookseller ever to preside over the renowned book-industry trade association the Cercle de la Librairie: after all, his store bridges the gap between tradition and modernity like almost no other such enterprise. "The Librarie Mollat has gained international fame thanks to the 'bookfaces' on our Instagram channel," says Emmanuelle Robillard, head of project and quality management. The historic bookstore's web presence ranges from podcasts and online radio to its own YouTube channel. "We put up recordings from the roughly 240 author events that we hold every year, for one thing," says Robillard.

The store's own events hub, Station Ausone, is a leading light in Bordeaux's cultural scene, hosting readings, concerts, and an ever-changing program of events. Some 55 booksellers work at the Librairie Mollat, read almost every book themselves, issue recommendations and advice, and plan and attend the many events. "Bookstores forge social connections. They're places for people to indulge their curiosity, slake their thirst for knowledge, and encounter writers, publishers, and institutions," says Robillard. "Every bookstore is a little world in itself."

223

EL ATENEO GRAND SPLENDID

BUENOS AIRES · ARGENTINA

Drama, baby: literature is showcased to perfection in this theater converted into a bookstore

With its crimson theater curtains and shimmering gold boxes, El Ateneo Grand Splendid must be one of the most spectacular bookstores in the world. Visitors browse through the large selection of titles to the strains of soft piano music: a pianist plays live, in an echo of the magnificent hall's previous life. The theater, which opened in 1903, initially put on classic stage shows, before being used as a cinema, radio studio, and tango hall, and finally reopening as a bookstore in 2000. Today, you can browse through books in the former boxes. What was once the stage has been transformed into a large reading area with an integrated café. The team regularly puts on popular readings and cultural events, which draw in literary greats like Rosa Montero, Paul Auster, and Mario Vargas Llosa, along with the many loyal regular customers. El Ateneo Grand Splendid has remained wonderfully true to itself and is still telling stories—just in a slightly different guise. 📖

TOP Giving books center stage: this bookstore's theatrical past is still very much apparent.

LEFT The inviting tiers and boxes have seen plenty of stories, whether on the stage or in books.

OPPOSITE Now a bookstore, the building was previously used as a theater, cinema, radio studio, and tango dance hall.

It's no surprise that El Ateneo Grand Splendid regularly features on lists
of the most beautiful bookstores in the world.

A KINGDOM OF SECONDHAND BOOKS

JOHN KING BOOKS · DETROIT · USA

No café or fripperies—just a million used books and some astounding rare editions in an industrial building with creaky floors and a legendary reputation

John King says his namesake store is still "*just a used bookstore*," even after fifty years—"and a parking lot!" The charismatic grand seigneur surveils the innumerable rows of shelving, greets browsing customers by name, and wipes imaginary dust from the spines of the volumes. John King Books—or, to give the store its full name, John K. King Used & Rare Books—is a Detroit institution. The four floors of this former glove factory house all kinds of works, from classics in every conceivable format to medieval parchments and leather-bound writings from all over the world.

Writer Hunter S. Thompson and music legend David Bowie both came here to buy books for their private collections. And King was there to sell them: "It is what I do, what I was meant to do, what I have always done." He leads us through the labyrinth of shelves to the Rare Book Room. Among 30,000 rare volumes contained in this room are a first-edition copy of *Treasure Island* by Scottish author Robert Louis Stevenson, dating from 1883, and a copy of *Pablo Escobar Gaviria en*

caricaturas 1983-1991, signed and fingerprinted by the Colombian drug lord himself. "It's insanely rare," comments King. "But I actually wanted to show you something else." With a mixture of pride and reverence, the expert takes a black folder out from beneath his desk and opens it up. "The Gutenberg [page] we have features the Gospel of Luke where Jesus is instructing his disciples on how to cast out demons. It's incredible to actually have a page from the world's first printed book."

Only around 180 copies of the Gutenberg Bible have survived to this day. As the very first book in the western world, it was predominantly printed with movable type. It's probably his favorite book of all, he says. "Not because of the content, but because it gave books to the masses. It made books accessible to anyone who can read. Before then, a book was like a piece of art, it was one-of-a-kind, and books were owned →

231

JOHN KING BOOKS

→ by very few people. Now, some 550 years later, try to find a home without a bookcase, a person who isn't in the middle of reading a book or two or three. Everyone's life has been touched by owning a book, holding a book, feeling a book in one's hands."

King is certainly no exception. John King Books was borne of his huge passion for books, strong collector's instinct, and sense of adventure. "Back in the old days, it was romanticized having a used bookstore," he says. "But the reality is you have to be tenacious. Running a successful bookstore goes by some, but not all, principles of business. I had no formal business education. Had to learn everything the hard way, had to learn by doing. I made all the classic rookie mistakes and even invented some new ones."

This apparently incongruous collision of worlds is one of the things that marks out John King Books as being so special. It is the industrial past cradling the creative future, the sharp business mind ensuring the persistence of the romantic, the new ensuring history's legacy.

The days when King used to sell books from the trunk of his '54 Packard are long gone. He bought the old glove factory in 1983. Today, the store is so huge that his employees communicate using walkie-talkies. Many staff members have been with John King Books for decades, having worked here since the 1980s. He still takes pleasure in the thought that he has been able to fill this once-vacant building with stories and ideas. "Of course, [books] are a commodity, to be bought and sold. They are also living things, each with a different personality, a different look, a different history. And, books are pieces of ourselves: a favorite book is a gift from one to another, telling more about oneself than any greeting card inscription." And speaking of greeting cards, the famous magician Teller sends a Christmas card every year declaring that John King Books is his favorite bookstore in the whole wide world. 📕

WRITER HUNTER S. THOMPSON AND MUSIC LEGEND DAVID BOWIE BOTH CAME HERE TO BUY BOOKS FOR THEIR PRIVATE COLLECTIONS.

LEFT Detroit is the adopted home of John King, here standing on the roof of his legendary bookstore.

OPPOSITE The team members, who communicate with one another using walkie-talkies, help visitors navigate their way through the countless aisles.

ATLANTIS BOOKS

OÍA · SANTORINI · GREECE

How a holiday daydream of two students became a convivial island bookstore with a view of the sea

TOP Penniless writers and artists are welcome to stay in the bookstore for a few days in return for helping out.

OPPOSITE The store has a gorgeous roof terrace with a few bookshelves and places to sit.

When the American students Oliver Wise and Craig Walzer went on vacation to Santorini in the spring of 2002, they soon discovered that while exquisite wine was readily available on the Greek island, there was nowhere to buy good books. They decided to return at some point and open their dream bookstore. Wise christened the idea Atlantis Books, and the friends chuckled at the idea that their children would one day take over the store.

After graduating from university, Wise and Walzer rounded up a few friends and set up on Santorini in early 2004. "We found an empty house in Oia, drank some whiskey, and signed a contract," recalls the team. "Before too long, we had a dog and a cat, opened an account, built a few shelves, and put some books in them." Atlantis Books opened in the spring of 2004. The shop's roof terrace looks right out over the deep, blue Mediterranean Sea. To this day, the bookstore, which is modeled on Shakespeare and Company in Paris, welcomes writers and artists from all over the world, "as long as they promise to make our bookstore a little bit more interesting." Over time, the team has acquired a second dog and adopted another cat. And they're still tickled at the notion that their children (who are now part of the team) might one day end up running the place. 📖

235

BOOKS AND
ALL THAT JAZZ

THE JAZZHOLE · LAGOS · NIGERIA

The unconventional blend of literature, jazz, and a café makes this independent bookstore a buzzing cultural hub

Lagos wouldn't be Lagos without The Jazzhole. The popular store selling books and vinyl has been providing stimulation in the Nigerian capital, which lies on the Atlantic coast, for almost 30 years. In the heart of the trendy Ikoyi neighborhood, the sandy yellow façade looks relatively unassuming, but behind it lies a glittering realm of literature and jazz. "We carry an incredible spread of books; a mix of old and new," says Tundun Tejuoso, who runs The Jazzhole together with her husband, Kunle Tejuoso. The shelves and tables are piled with Nigerian and international fiction, antiquarian treasures, and specialist publications. Coffee-table books, comics, and fashion magazines complete the section. The bestselling novel *Americanah* by the Nigerian writer Chimamanda Ngozi Adichie is prominently displayed alongside other popular titles, not least because it includes a particularly glowing mention of The Jazzhole.

Kunle Tejuoso opened The Jazzhole in 1991 as an offshoot of the independent Nigerian bookstore chain Glendora Books, which had been founded by his mother, Gbemisola Tejuoso, in 1975. "He grew up on books and had a strong passion for music from a young age," says Tundun Tejuoso. "He graduated with a master's in electrical engineering in New York and returned immediately to Lagos to Glendora in the late 1980s. He opened The Jazzhole a few years afterwards." Kunle Tejuoso's vision was to open a bookstore that would serve as a platform for contemporary culture, literature, and jazz from all over the world. Its character has always made the store different and very unlike the conventional bookstores in this part of the world; it might sound unconventional, but it has proven to be a huge success. The selection of books and range of vinyl dovetail brilliantly. Uncontested greats like Miles Davis and Bob Marley are ranged →

LEFT One of Tundun Tejuoso's employees helps out in the bookstore café, which opened in the early 2000s.

OPPOSITE The wooden shelves of The Jazzhole are stuffed with new and secondhand novels, non-fiction books, comics, and magazines.

237

THE JAZZHOLE

LEFT Classical instruments and photographs of renowned Nigerian and international jazz maestros adorn the walls.

BOTTOM The books on sale at The Jazzhole range from international best-sellers to Nigerian literature.

OPPOSITE The popular book-store serves up the finest jazz together with African coffee and vegan carrot cake.

OVER THE YEARS, THE JAZZHOLE HAS BECOME AN ICONIC LANDMARK RELEVANT TO ALL AGES.

→ alongside recordings by local and national artists like Afrobeat musician Duro Ikujenyo and the French-Nigerian singer and songwriter Aṣa. "Our music collection is as deep as you can think," says Tundun Tejuoso. "CDs and vinyl from the 'freest' of jazz to the latest in new African/Afro-diasporic forms, with a strong specialization in traditional and modern Nigerian music."

In the early 2000s, the store was joined by a small café, where guests sit at little wooden tables reading and relaxing to the strains of soft jazz music, over African coffee and vegan carrot cake. In addition, the couple hosts well-attended readings, movie screenings, concerts, and jam sessions at which artists and the audience party

between the bookshelves and stacks of vinyl. "Over the years, The Jazzhole has become an iconic landmark relevant to all ages," says Tundun delightedly. She describes the store as an oasis for the mind. "[Places like this] are so necessary, in a fast-growing megapolis such as Lagos—where everybody is on the hustle to become someone in life." 📖

239

TOP Part of the Jazzhole's charm also comes from the works of art on display and the plethora of little curiosities.

LEFT Once a jazz fan, always a jazz fan. A browse through the colossal vinyl collection can turn up some rare finds.

OPPOSITE Venerable jazz legends watch over the office, which is brimming with literature and inspiration.

LIVRARIA LELLO

PORTO · PORTUGAL

This historic bookstore is so famous that lines now form and visitors pay an entrance fee

W as *Harry Potter* author J. K. Rowling really inspired by this bookstore? Standing on the velvety red staircase and gazing out over the gorgeous Livraria Lello, you could well imagine that you've arrived at Hogwarts School of Witchcraft and Wizardry. The famous bookstore, which invariably ranks as one of the most beautiful in the world, has stood here since 1881. José Manuel Lello is a member of the fifth generation to run the business. He also keeps pace with rapid changes, even if under duress.

His bookstore started receiving hordes of tourists every day. They mostly came just to take selfies and left without buying any books. By 2015, the Livraria Lello was teetering on the brink of bankruptcy. Following extensive discussions, Lello and his team therefore came to an unprecedented decision: they would have to ask for a small entrance fee in order to save the store. The policy was implemented without further ado. This reasonable fee did nothing to diminish the popularity of the legendary bookstore. Just like before, visitors still line up →

RIGHT The bookstore's stairs are thought to have inspired *Harry Potter* author J. K. Rowling.

OPPOSITE There are often lines of visitors eager to get a glimpse behind the enchanting façade of the Livraria Lello.

243

→ expectantly in front of the neo-Gothic façade in the Rua das Carmelitas. The entrance fee is credited in full toward the purchase of any book. As clever and as adaptive as Hermione brewing Polyjuice Potion, the books on sale at the Livraria Lello are now strongly geared towards the largely tourist clientele. Along with Portuguese literature, English, French, Spanish, and Italian books pack the shelves, while postcards, travel guides, and little souvenirs supplement the wares on sale. And it goes without saying that the *Harry Potter* books have pride of place. 📖

TOP The range of books in the historic shelves has moved with the times and is now geared towards an international clientele.

OPPOSITE The exquisitely beautiful bookstore is one of the most popular sights in the Portuguese city of Porto.

245

LIVRARIA LELLO

TOP With velvety red carpet on top and rich wooden ornamentation below, the stairs of the Livraria Lello are a work of art in themselves.

LEFT Books have been ringing the cash register since 1881—and so, since 2015, have entry fees.

OPPOSITE Visitors who do more than just take selfies can redeem their entry fee against any book purchase.

With its finely carved wooden shelves and majestic staircase,
the Livraria Lello is a fairytale bookstore.

AS WE ALL KNOW, IN THE BEGINNING WAS THE WORD

BOEKHANDEL DOMINICANEN · MAASTRICHT · NETHERLANDS

If there's a heaven for book lovers, then the hallowed aisles and hushed galleries of this Gothic church in Maastricht might well be it

Ton Harmes and his team are the guardians of these sacred halls. Behind the monumental doorway to the Boekhandel Dominicanen, the old Gothic church is stuffed with classical and scholarly literature, international magazines and newspapers, and a huge selection of music. Warm light streams in through the ancient windows, falling upon the colossal modern steel shelves. Between them, book lovers wander up and down in search of inspiration. Business is booming at what is now one of the world's most popular bookstores, but that was once far from a foregone conclusion. Having been at risk of bankruptcy, the store was luckily able to avoid closing altogether thanks to the people of Maastricht, explains Harmes. A crowdfunding campaign raised over 100,000 Euros within just seven days to keep the bookstore going.

The campaign really welded Harmes's team and the store's tribe of loyal customers together. The local people remember the once-disastrous condition of the church only too well. "It was used as a bicycle shed and snake exhibition →

BOEKHANDEL DOMINICANEN

LEFT Ton Harmes has transformed this old church into a much-loved bookstore, café, and cultural hub.

OPPOSITE The straight steel shelving is visually restrained, so that the impressive Gothic architecture remains center-stage.

BOOKS ARE MADE TO TAKE HOME, TO ENJOY, TO CHALLENGE, TO BE THERE FOR YOU WHENEVER YOU WANT OR NEED THEM.

→ [center] at the same time," recalls Harmes. Maastricht City Council was delighted when the bookseller and his team submitted their plans for giving the church a new lease on life. Today, Boekhandel Dominicanen is a much-loved bookstore, café, and cultural hub for this Dutch university town. Together with conventional book launches and signings, the vast nave also hosts classical, jazz, and pop concerts, dance performances, debates, parties, and dinner events. During the day, heavenly cappuccinos are served in what was once the sanctuary. Books have a certain aura about them, enthuses Harmes, and

"the aura of the book shines on the booksellers as well." Being able to make customers happy, he says, is "wonderful." The seasoned book dealer surveys his realm from the steel gallery. "Books are made to take home, to enjoy, to challenge, to be there for you whenever you want or need them," he says. Books like *Battle Cry,* the debut novel by U. S. writer Leon Uris; the bestselling *Noble House,* by British-American author James Clavell; or *De Wereldomwandelaar* [in English, *The Man who Walked the World Around*], by the Dutch philosopher Govert Derix, are the reason why he does this job: "Some [books] are my best friends." 📖

Visitors can enjoy a heavenly cappuccino in what was once
the altar area and the site of sermons.

DAIKANYAMA TSUTAYA BOOKS

TOKYO · JAPAN

This prize-winning feat of architecture
houses an astounding selection of books
over three floors

TOP The façade of this oversized bookstore, made of interlocking Ts, is already an iconic sight.

OPPOSITE Together with its large selection of books, Daikanyama Tsutaya Books also has an international music and film department.

Daikanyama Tsutaya Books is often described as the "book empire" of the Japanese capital, and not without reason: the enormous bookstore is hugely inviting despite its sheer size, and it offers a vast selection of books for visitors to lose themselves among. As the beating heart of the prize-winning Daikanyama T-Site, the bookstore is also a must-see for any architecture enthusiast. The studio Klein Dythamw architecture won prizes for the tripartite building, which is formed from interlocking Ts and features a highly distinctive façade, including at the World Architecture Festival in 2013. Inside, mostly Japanese and English-language fiction and specialist literature await, together with a large movie and music department, a superb selection of stationery—with a particular emphasis on Japanese paper—and a top-notch café and restaurant. The T-Site also hosts regular pop-up markets that prove to be a magnet for Tokyo's cultural scene, with visitors invariably ending up browsing the latest additions to the book displays. 📖

257

DAIKANYAMA TSUTAYA BOOKS

TOP The bookstore is also prized for its international magazines on everything from architecture and fashion to nature.

LEFT: Daikanyama Tsutaya Books is built on books themselves: the layered boards make a superb place to read and work.

OPPOSITE The studio Klein Dytham architecture won a coveted award for its design for the complex.

259

BOOKS OVER THE CLOUDS

SHANGHAI · CHINA

At a towering 239 meters, this symbol-laden temple to design is the highest bookstore in China

The name of this bookstore is far from an exaggeration: Books over the Clouds looks out over a Chinese megacity from the 52nd floor of the Shanghai Tower. The Duoyun Books flagship store opened in mid-August 2019 and is already a firm fixture on the list of must-see sights for Shanghai locals and tourists alike. "On its first day, enthusiastic visitors had to wait for three hours before they could take the elevator of the tallest skyscraper in the country to reach the bookstore, 239 meters above the ground floor," says Public Relations Manager He Xiaomin. The striking design is the work of the Shanghai-based firm of architects Wutopia Lab. "The sky and the city should be part of the design of the bookstore," explains the team. Some 100 laborers toiled over the fittings for 60 days, →

RIGHT The architecture is defined by the broad arches that run though many areas of the bookstore.

OPPOSITE The Chinese supercity stretches from the Shanghai Tower all the way to the horizon.

→ working from 300 drawings. Lifting 260 tons of shelving units into the space required 150 laborers, whereupon it took ten days to build them. Finally, thirty-five store employees spent four days slotting 60,000 books into the shelves. The expansive space includes an exhibition area, a café, and the bright Douban High Score Book Area, which stands opposite the dark green-painted London Book Review Bookstore Area. "One section represents the East, one represents the West," say the architects; they are "interdependent and competing with each other." Sometimes you can feel the love, sometimes not, they say, but in a sense, our world is all about East and West. 📖

TOP The mirrored pillar reflects the combination of skyline and bookshelves.

OPPOSITE Sheer vertigo: the dizzying view from the window plunges more than 780 feet down.

263

BOOKS OVER THE CLOUDS

TOP The Shanghai-based architectural firm Wutopia Lab designed the stunning interior of the bookstore.

LEFT Books over the Clouds is the flagship store of Duoyan Books. The in-house café makes a superb place to read and relax.

OPPOSITE The arches and aisles create a succession of inviting nooks, while also providing a structure for the range of books.

INDEX

BRAZENHEAD BOOKS

New York City, USA
brazenheadbooks.com
Photography:
Samir Abady (pp. 102, 104, 106 top),
Gracie Bialecki (p. 103),
Alex Brook Lynn (pp. 105,
106 bottom, 107)

CAFEBRERÍA EL PÉNDULO

Alejandro Dumas 81,
Polanco, Polanco IV Secc,
Miguel Hidalgo,
11560 Ciudad de México,
Mexico
pendulo.com
Photography:
Jaime Nauarro Soto (pp. 24–27)

CĂRTUREŞTI CARUSEL

Strada Lipscani 55,
Bucharest 030033, Romania
carturesti.ro
Photography:
Cosmin Dragomir (pp. 214–217)

CASA BOSQUES

Córdoba 25, Roma Nte.,
Cuauhtémoc,
06700 Ciudad de México,
Mexico
casabosques.net
Photography:
Juan Hernández (p. 148),
Courtesy of Casa Bosques
(pp. 149, 151),
Alejandro Cartagena (p. 150)

CINNOBER

Landemærket 9,
1119 Copenhagen K,
Denmark
cinnoberbookshop.dk
Photography:
Jan Søndergaard (pp. 166–167)

CITY LIGHTS BOOKSELLERS & PUBLISHERS

261 Columbus Ave, San
Francisco, CA 94133, USA
citylights.com
Photography:
Lisa Kimura (pp. 208–213)

COOK & BOOK

Place du Temps Libre 1,
1200 Woluwe-Saint-Lambert,
Brussels, Belgium
cookandbook.be
Photography:
„By 2 Photographers" (pp. 38–43)

DAIKANYAMA TSUTAYA BOOKS

16–15 Sarugakucho, Shibuya City,
Tokyo 150–0033, Japan
tsutaya.tsite.jp
Photography:
Nacása & Partners (pp. 256–259)

DESPERATE LITERATURE

Calle de Campomanes, 13,
28013 Madrid, Spain
desperateliterature.com
Photography:
Courtesy of Desperate
Literature (pp. 110–111, 112 top,
113–115),
Sergio Gonzáles Valero/
EL MUNDO (p. 112 bottom)

DO YOU READ ME?!

Auguststraße 28,
10117 Berlin, Germany
doyoureadme.de
Photography:
Jannick Børlum (pp. 8, 10 bottom),
Schmott (pp. 9, 10 top, 11)

DYSLEXIA LIBROS

1a Ave Sur, #11,
Antigua, Guatemala
Photography:
Daniel López Pérez (p. 92),
Polina Molchaova (pp. 93–95)

EL ATENEO GRAND SPLENDID

Av. Santa Fe 1860, C1123 CABA,
Buenos Aires, Argentina
yenny-elateneo.com/local/grand-splendid
Photography:
Diego Grandi/Alamy (p. 224),
Rosal Rene Betancourt 9/Alamy (p. 225),
Jeff Greenberg/Alamy (p. 226 top),
Jeffrey Isaac Greenberg 6/
Alamy (p. 226 bottom),
Andrew Palmer/Alamy (p. 227),
Grupo Ilhsa S. A. (pp. 228–229)

FILBOOKS

Kemankeş Karamustafa Paşa,
Ali Paşa Değirmeni Sk. 1/1,
34425 Beyoğlu/İstanbul, Turkey
filbooks.net
Photography:
Depikt (pp. 12, 14 top, 15),
Cemre Yeşil Gönenli (pp. 13,
14 bottom)

GOLDEN HARE BOOKS

68 St Stephen St, Stockbridge,
Edinburgh EH3 5AQ,
United Kingdom
goldenharebooks.com
Photography:
Sarah Cooke (p.108)

HALPER'S BOOKS

Allenby Street 87
Tel Aviv-Yafo IL 62489,
Israel
halpers-books.business.site
Photography:
Yoni Lerner (p. 160),
Courtesy of Halper's Books
(pp. 161–163)

HAPPY VALLEY

294 Smith St,
Collingwood VIC 3066,
Melbourne, Australia
happyvalleyshop.com
Photography:
Kristoffer Paulsen (pp. 124–125)

HONESTY BOOKSHOP

Hay-on-Wye,
United Kingdom
haycastletrust.org/visitus
Photography:
Loop Images Ltd/Alamy (p. 68),
Andrew Fox/Alamy (p. 69),
Homer Sykes/Alamy (p. 70 top),
Steven May/Alamy (p. 70 bottom),
Haydn Pugh/Honesty Bookshop (p. 71),
Jeff Morgan 03/Alamy (pp. 72–73)

INDEX

PRO QM
Almstadtstraße 48,
10119 Berlin, Germany
pro-qm.de
Photography:
Katja Eydel (pp. 140, 142, 143),
Courtesy of Pro qm (p. 141)

READINGS
309 Lygon St, Carlton
VIC 3053, Australia
readings.com.au
Photography:
Chris Middleton (pp. 126–127)

SCARTHIN
BOOKS
The Promenade, Cromford,
Matlock DE4 3QF,
United Kingdom
scarthinbooks.com
Photography:
Courtesy of Scarthin Books
(pp. 56–57)

SHAKESPEARE
& COMPANY
37 Rue de la Bûcherie,
75005 Paris, France
shakespeareandcompany.com
Photography:
Bruno De Hogues/
getty images (p. 129),
David Grove (pp. 130, 135),
Kiren (131 top),
Bonnie Elliot (p. 134),
Miguel Medina/
getty images (p. 131 bottom),
Hulton Archive/
getty images (p. 132),
John van Hasselt – Corbis/
getty images (p. 133)

STRAND
BOOKSTORE
828 Broadway, New York,
NY 10003, USA
strandbooks.com
Photography:
Courtesy of Strand
Bookstore (pp. 84, 85 top),
Janna Jesson/Strand
Bookstore (pp. 85 bottom,
87 top),
Alexander Alland, Jr./
getty images (p. 86),
Colleen Callery/Strand
Bookstore (p. 87 bottom)

THE BOOK BARGE
Port de Chitry – Chaumot,
Chitry-les-Mines 58800, France
thebookbarge.com
Photography:
Sarah Henshaw (pp. 58–63)

THE JAZZHOLE
168 Awolowo Rd, Ikoyi,
Lagos, Nigeria
Photography:
Ginikachi Eloka
(pp. 236–238, 240–241),
Adey Omotade (p. 239)

THE RIPPED
BODICE
3806 Main St, Culver City,
CA 90232, USA
herippedbodicela.com
Photography:
Jenn LeBlanc (pp. 156–159)

THE WRITER'S
BLOCK
519 S 6th St #100, Las Vegas,
NV 89101, USA
thewritersblock.org
Photography:
Emily Wilson (pp. 32–35)

TREADWELL'S
33 Store St, Bloomsbury,
London WC1E 7BS,
United Kingdom
treadwells-london.com
Photography:
Londonstills.com/Alamy (p. 194),
Karolina Heller (pp. 195–199)

UNDER THE
COVER
R. Marquês Sá da Bandeira 88B,
1050–060 Lisbon, Portugal
underthecover.pt
Photography:
Courtesy of Under the Cover (p. 164),
Hugo Amaral (p. 165)

VVG
SOMETHING
Da'an District,
Taipei City, Taiwan
Photography:
Courtesy of VVG Something
(pp. 118–121)

WILD RUMPUS
2720 W 43rd St,
Minneapolis,
MN 55410, USA
wildrumpusbooks.com
Photography:
Drew Sieplinga
(p. 146 top left, bottom),
David Luke (pp. 146 top right, 147)

WUGUAN
BOOKS
2–1, Da Yi St.,
Yancheng District,
Kaohsiung City, Taiwan
Photography:
Lee Kuo-Min (pp. 152–155)

Do You Read Me?

Bookstores Around The World

This book was conceived, edited, and designed by gestalten.

Contributing editor: Marianne Julia Strauss

Edited by Robert Klanten and Maria-Elisabeth Niebius

Preface by Juergen Boos

Texts by Marianne Julia Strauss, except for pp. 44–47 by Jen Campbell, pp. 88–91 by Fiona Killackey, pp. 136–139 by Alison Flood

Translation from German to English by Maisie Fitzpatrick in association with First Edition Translations Ltd, Cambridge, UK

Editorial management by Lars Pietzschmann

Cover, design and layout by Stefan Morgner
Layout assistance by Johanna Posiege

Photo editor: Madeline Dudley-Yates

Typefaces: Saol Text by Florian Schick and Lauri Toikka and Editorial New by Mathieu Desjardins

Cover illustration by Marc Martin

Backcover images by FiLBooks (left), Books Are Magic (top right), Book Therapy/Mischa Babel (middle left), Cărturești Carusel/Cosmin Dragomir (middle right), Cafebrería El Péndulo/Eduardo Aizenman (bottom right)
Endpapers illustrations by Johanna Posiege

Printed by Grafisches Centrum Cuno, Calbe (Saale)

Made in Germany

Published by gestalten, Berlin 2020

ISBN 978-3-89955-994-1

2nd printing, 2020

For more information, and to order books, please visit www.gestalten.com

Bibliographic information published by the Deutsche Nationalbibliothek.

The Deutsche Nationalbibliothek lists this publication in the Deutsche Nationalbibliografie;

detailed bibliographic data is available online at www.dnb.de

None of the content in this book was published in exchange for payment by commercial parties or designers; gestalten selected all included work based solely on its artistic merit.

This book was printed on paper certified according to the standards of the FSC®.

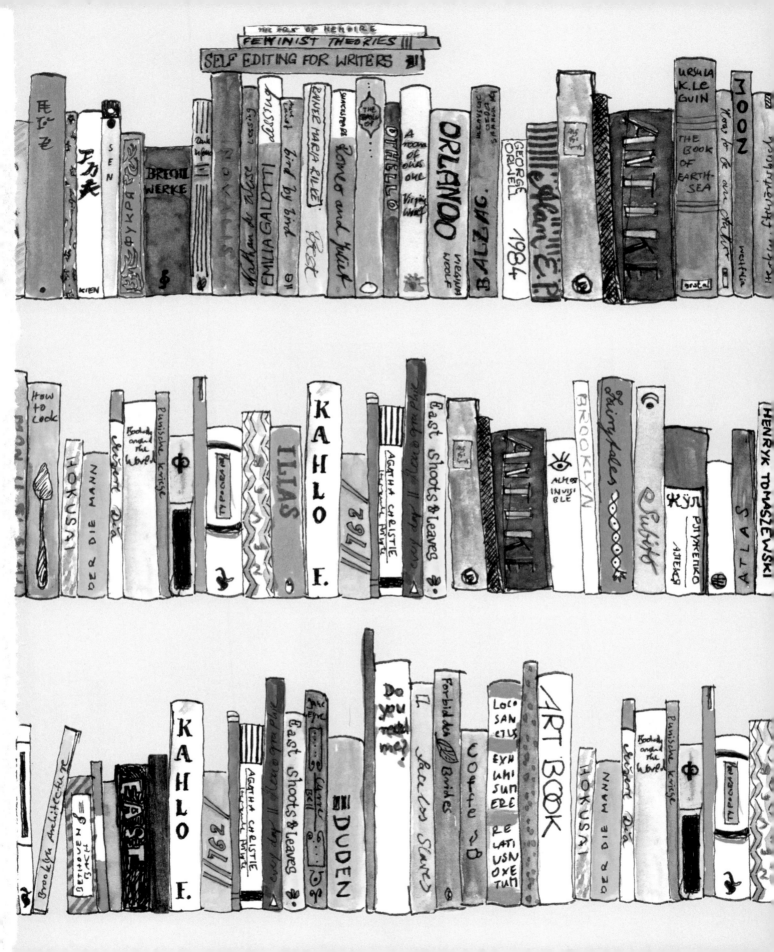